The Book of
CRAFT BEERDS

A well-groomed collection of craft beer labels by

Fred Abercrombie

Photography and design by Tyler Warrender and David Hodges

INTEGRATED ADVERTISING

The Craft Beerds Book
www.craftbeerds.com

A creation of ABERCROMBIE+ALCHEMY
Integrated Advertising
www.abertising.com

ISBN-13: 9781937359379

Distributed by Cameron + Company, Petaluma, CA
www.cameronbooks.com

Printed and bound in China by Global PSD
www.globalpsd.com

ABERCROMBIE+ALCHEMY & Global Printing, Sourcing & Development (Global PSD), in association with American Forests and the Global ReLeaf programs, will plant two trees for each tree used in the manufacturing of this book. Global ReLeaf is an international campaign by American Forests, the nation's oldest nonprofit conservation organization and a world leader in planting trees for environmental restoration.

Replanted Paper

Special Thanks to our KICKSTARTERS

You would not be holding this fine-follicled tome without the generosity of our Kickstarter backers—only some of which are listed here.

If you're not familiar, Kickstarter.com is a site that lets you essentially pitch your creative idea to the world. You set a financial goal of what you need to get going and if enough people pledge donations within your allotted time, you get funded. If you don't reach your goal in time, you don't get squat.

We managed to finish at 134% funding (woo-hoo!). While that only covered half our actual print costs, it made printing a hell of a lot more possible. So to all who contributed, I owe you a beer. Which I will gladly buy on Tuesday. Thank you so very much.

ACE DISTRIBUTING
AHARON & MARVA SOMERVILLE
ALEX LENTZ
ALICE AND BRIAN CARAWAY
ALLE AND DAVID AUFDERHAAR
AMY LIU
ANDREW WOLF
ARLENE BAE
BEGYLE BREWING
BEN LOVE
BERT MAYER
BETH POLEY
BRAD "THEBIGBEATDOWN" SPIKER
BRAD KONKLE
BRAD WARRENDER
BRENDAN GORMLEY
BRIAN WAY
BRYCE BUSLER
CANDY RIDDELL
CARL GLASS
CAROLINE JAUCH
CHAD LOTHIAN
CHARLES V PARKER
CHRIS GRUENER
CHRIS "THE NOEISH" NOE
CHRIS & ERIN SCOTT
CHRIS BREDESEN
CHRIS FORESTA
CHRIS HOANG
CHRIS VIBBERTS
COAST BREWING CO.

COLBY CURTIS
COLIN ROBISON
CRAIG AND CARRIE BUCKLES
CROOKED FENCE BREWING CO
CRUSTY LOCAL BREWING COMPANY
D & E LASIEWSKI
DAMON GREGG / GREATBEARD BREWHAUS
DANIEL ÅBERG
DAVID ROGERS
DICK TERPSTRA
DONNA M. SMITH
DOUGLAS J. BROWN
DRAUGHT BOARD
DYLAN JAMES HO
ED CLEARY
EINAT RAN
EMMA RIVKAH JEROME: MISS MUSTACHIO
FRAN SLED
GABE KEARNEY
GNOFF
GODFATHER SUPREME FRED FREY
GREG HELLER-LABELLE
GREG OVERLEY
IAN LEAHY
JACK & PEGGY
JAMES GRANT
JAMES GREENE
JAN BOLINDER
JASON SELLERS
JAY REDD
JAY SOKOLOFF

Choose from
POPULAR BEERD STYLES. . .

FOREWORD

Really? A whole book on this?

Well, I've got a question for you: Ever been to a beer fest or brewery? You can't swing a growler without grazing a beard. Maybe it's in the water. Maybe it's in the fact that I'm swingin' growlers in crowds. To me it just makes sense.

Take a look at the beer shelf next time you're at the store. Or rather, stop reading and take a look at the rest of this book. Who reads Forewords anyway?

North Coast's Old Rasputin and Coney Island's Human Blockhead were the first to grab my eyeballs. Then all the many variations of Rogue 'staches made me realize there was something furry afoot. The more I looked, the more beerds I found.

Your favorite bottle shop probably has plenty of classic Euro Beerds to geek out on—the Moretti man and Samichlaus come to mind—but I wanted to focus on the design and creativity of modern craft beers in America (plus a few strays from our Canadian neighbors). These are the hairy faces of breweries inspiring all-new growth back in Europe and all across the globe. I also wanted to highlight some of the many, little regional breweries you may never find on shelves near you.

As for myself, I'm only a part-time bearder. Every year, on July 4th, I declare my independence from shaving and grow all the way until the annual Petaluma Whiskerino in October; which my wife and I have helped run and promote for years. And if I didn't love kissing her so much I'd probably grow year-round. Thankfully I can get my follicle fix on shelves or at the next growler fill.

So, answering your question: Yes, really. And I hope you enjoy it as much as I have. Really.

Cheers,

Fred

§01

I thought the best place to start this collection of modern Craft Beerd labels was with the breweries that pay tribute to their lineage. Mostly brewers from eras when facial hair was super prevalent. Now in 2012 the two topics are tangled together once again. Hirsute history repeated.

Photo-Illustrations by David Hodges/DNK Digital | dnkdigital.com

Anaheim Brewing Company
Anaheim, CA
anaheimbrew.com

Anaheim Hefeweizen is a traditional German-style wheat beer. We use a special yeast to give our Hefeweizen a subtle clove aroma and a fruity hint of banana. Our label features Bavarian-born Anaheim resident Friedrich Conrad, who founded his "Anaheim Brewery" in 1888.

WHERE THE PAST
HAS PRESENCE.

Brewed and bottled by

Anaheim
HEFEWEIZEN

Roy Pitz Brewing Company | Chambersburg, PA | roypitz.com

"This dark brew was inspired by the historical Civil War burning of our hometown of Chambersburg, PA in July 1864. During the raid, Ludwig's Brewery, operated by George Ludwig II, was burned to the ground by Confederate soldiers under Gen. McCausland's orders. In remembrance of this truly buzz-killing event, we created a German style Rauchbier, or dark smoked lager. This beer uses all its ingredients from Bamberg, Germany, which is where the style was born (coincidentally, the same area where Ludwig himself was born and taught to brew)."

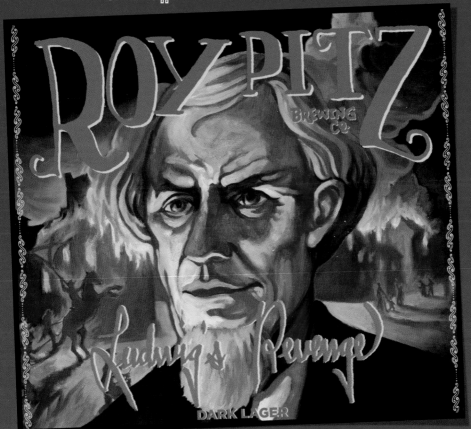

This is the face of Fred Gray, Founder of America's oldest family-owned beverage company. Since 1856.

Gray's Brewing Company
Janesville, WI
graybrewing.com

"The two gents are my grandfather John Elliott's grandfathers, making them my great-great grandfathers on my Mom's side of the family. The one on the left side is named John Elliott, and the one on the right is named Michael Cary. They were both from Ireland, and they both worked for the railroads based in West Chicago, IL. The picture is taken at around the turn of the century on the front porch of one of their houses in West Chicago. My understanding is that they were best friends and in-laws, and spent much time hanging out on the front porch together, chewing tobacco. Supposedly, John taught Michael how to read in their later years, as he had been illiterate for much of his life. You can't see it in the picture, but Michael was missing a finger that he lost when coupling two trains together ... They also were not drinkers."

—*Mike Kainz,* OWNER & FOUNDER

Wild Onion Brewery | Lake Barrington, IL | onionpub.com

While not Forebrewers per se, they are forefathers.
And any beer that pays tribute to past relatives who didn't even drink,
especially with chin curtains like these, gets a cheers from me.

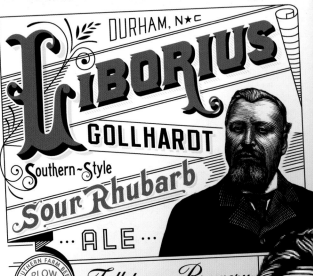

DURHAM, N★C

LIBORIUS

GOLLHARDT

Southern~Style

Sour Rhubarb

... ALE ...

SOUTHERN FARM BEER
**PLOW
= 2 =
PINT
★**

Fullsteam Brewery

12 FL OZ & 5.5 AB

Beer label and certificate art
by Kurt Lightner and design
by Christian Helms of Helms
Workshop
helmsworkshop.com

Yours truly
L. Gollhardt

FULLSTEAM BREWERY

SOUTHERN SOCIETY OF AWESOME · MEMBER · DURHAM, NORTH CAROLINA

LOYAL **ADMIRAL** LEADER

OFFICIALLY SANCTIONED

CERTIFICATE OF Awesome

PATRICK MARTIN

CERTIFIED AWESOME BY WRIT AND DECREE ON *August 13, 2010*

SCYTHE & SPARROW

Fullsteam Brewery | Durham, NC | http://fullsteam.ag

These Certificates of Awesome are part of Fullsteam's fundraising initiative to help build their on-site tavern. Donate a certain amount and they'll immortalize you on one of 'em. Once the tavern's complete, they'll hang—where else—on the tavern's Wall of Awesome.

As for Forebrewer Liborious Gollhardt here, he was actually the great-great grandfather of Fullsteam's head brewer, Chris Davis. Liborious himself was either a brewer or brewery director (the records are fuzzy, no pun intended) at E. Tosetti Brewing Company—a Chicago-based pre-prohibition brewery well-known for its Berliner Weisse beers. Pretty awesome lineage.

§02

Beard Team USA and the World Beard & Moustache Championships break 'staches into six categories: Natural, English, Dali, Imperial, Hungarian, and Freestyle. Since beer labels don't follow the same rules, we've grouped the following labels into a catch-all of miscellaneous lip liners. See if you can classify 'em yourself. Visit craftbeerds.com for help on style descriptions.

Photo-Illustrations by David Hodges/DNK Digital | dnkdigital.com

CURIOUS
TRAVELER
SHANDY
-ALE BREWED WITH LEMON PEEL-
-AND NATURAL FLAVORS ADDED-

12 FL OZ OF

The House of Shandy Beer Co. | Burlington, VT | houseofshandy.com

Curiously Pictured: Alan Newman
President, Alchemy & Science

Quite a Refresher!™

TENACIOUS

TRAVELER

SHANDY

12 FL OZ OF
— ALE BREWED WITH LEMON PEEL —
WITH NATURAL FLAVORS, HONEY, & GINGER ADDED

SEP 2012 | OCT 2012 | NOV 2012 | DEC 2012 | JAN 2013 | FEB 2013 | MAR 2013 | APR 2013 | MAY 2013 | JUN 2013 | JUL 2013 | AUG 2013

For the freshest experience, enjoy before the notched date.

BREWED AND BOTTLED BY
HOUSE OF SHANDY BEER COMPANY,
CINCINNATI, OH.

9126

Quite a Refresher!

Muskoka Brewery
Bracebridge, Ontario, Canada
muskokabrewery.com

QUALITY CRAFTED SINCE 1994

BREWER'S STACHE

highland
BREWING COMPANY

ASHEVILLE • NORTH CAROLINA

Baron Von Hopper

1 PINT 6 FL. OZ.

ALC. 6.3% BY VOL.

BEL... ...LE ALE

The Smuttynose BIG BEER Series

Homunculus
A Belgian Syle Golden Ale

MUTTYNOSE
BREWING Co.

• The Smuttynose Big Beer Series: big beers in big bottles, released seasonally in very limited quantities.
• After years of gestation our highly regarded hoppy Belgian style ale, "The Gnome" has been reborn as Homunculus. Impregnated with loads of hop character, balanced with malt sweetness & fruit esters derived from the Belgian yeast, this golden colored ale is ripe for the picking.
• Share some responsibly with your gnomies.

BREWED & BOTTLED BY SMUTTYNOSE BREWING CO.
PORTSMOUTH, NH • WWW.SMUTTYNOSE.COM

Highland Brewing Company
Asheville, NC
highlandbrewing.com

Smuttynose Brewing Company
Portsmouth, NH
smuttynose.com

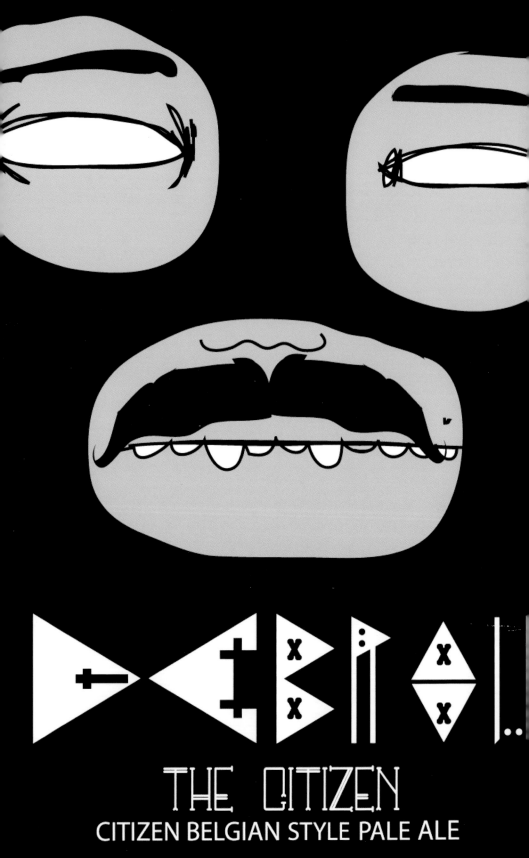

THE CITIZEN

CITIZEN BELGIAN STYLE PALE ALE

Dick's

DICK'S BEER

Dick's Brewing Company
Centralia, WA
dicksbeer.com

BEER 'Staches

Imperial Stout

Dick's Bre...

East End Brewing Company
Pittsburgh, PA
eastendbrewing.com

Artist: Vince Dorse
vincedorse.com

DC Brau Brewing Company
Washington, DC
dcbrau.com

Artist: Kelly Towles
kellytowles.com

Illustration Ale

BREWED AND BOTTLED BY
EAST END BREWING CO.
PITTSBURGH PA

NET CONTENTS: 1 QUART, 1.8 FL. OZ (1 LITRE)

FLOYD'S FOLLY
SCOTTISH ALE

NUT CRACKER ALE

BOULEVARD BREWING CO

Boulevard Brewing Company
Kansas City, MO
boulevard.com

Cutters Brewing Co.
Bloomington, IN
cuttersbrewing.com

Artist: Kurtis Beavers
kurtisbeavers.com

BELL'S®

ECCENTRIC ALE 2011
BREWED UNDER THE DISCERNING EYE OF LARRY.
MALT BEVERAGE BREWED WITH SPICES,
MAPLE SYRUP AND PERSIMMONS

BREWED AND BOTTLED BY
BELL'S BREWERY, INC., COMSTOCK, MI 49053

Bell's Brewery
Galesburg, MI
bellsbeer.com

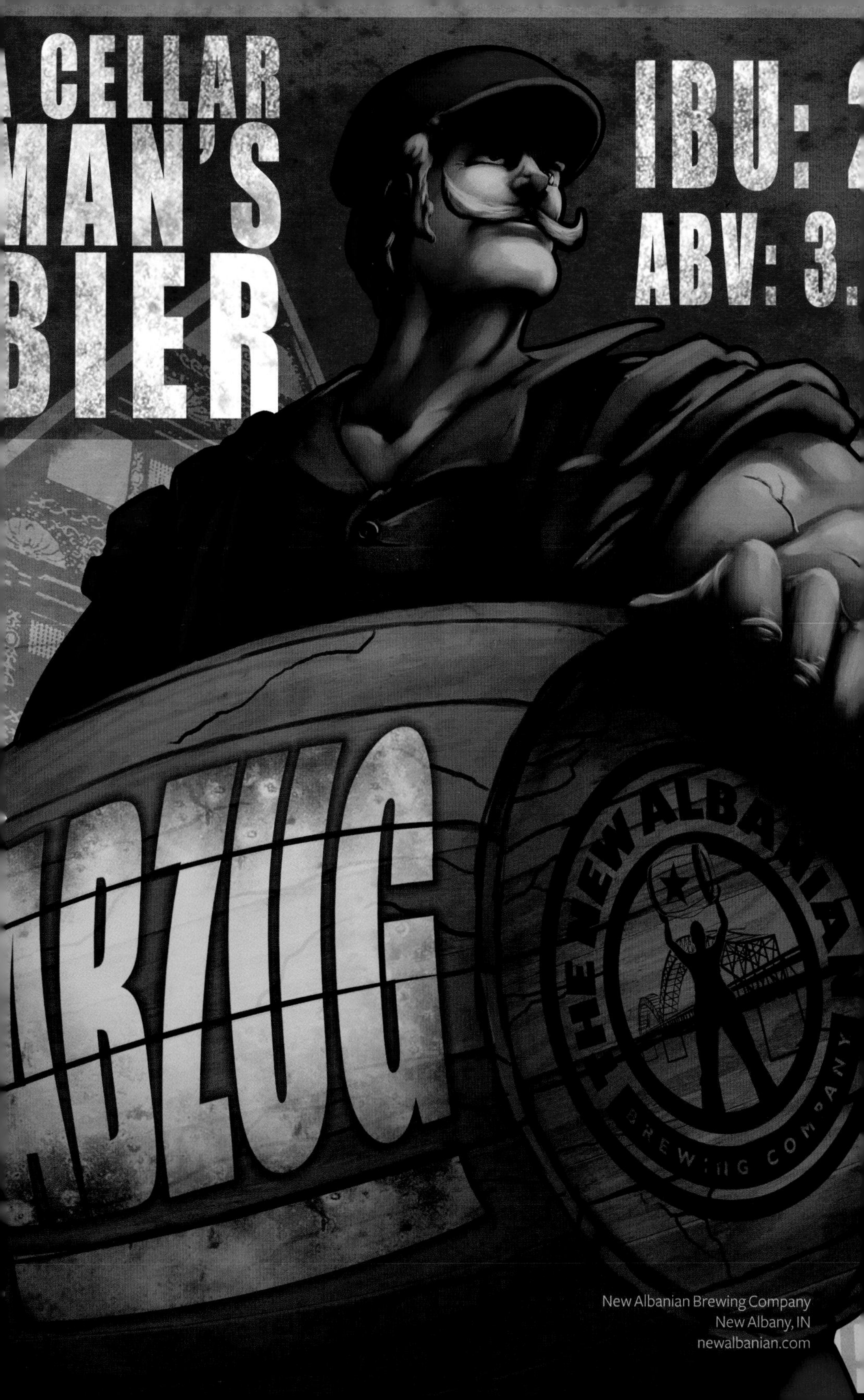
CELLAR
MAN'S
IBU:
ABV: 3.
THE NEW ALBANIAN
BREWING COMPANY
New Albanian Brewing Company
New Albany, IN
newalbanian.com

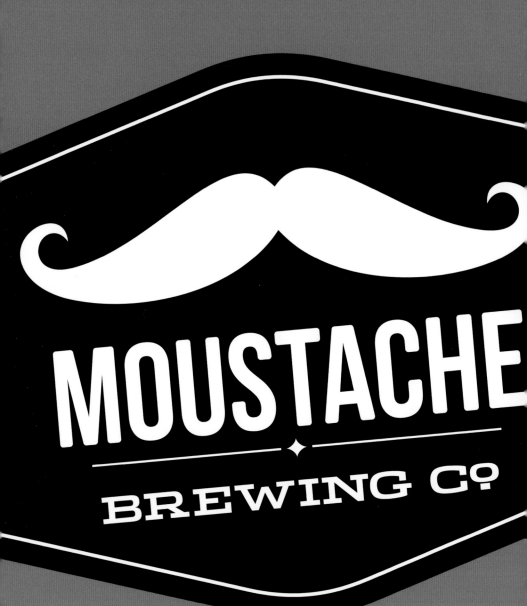

Moustache Brewing Co. | Long Island, NY | moustachebrewing.com

Tallgrass Brewing Company
Manhattan, KS
tallgrassbeer.com

the Bollocks

IMPERIAL INDIA PALE ALE

Brash Brewing | Houston, TX | brashbeers.com
Artist: Richard Bailey | additiveinverse.com

Monday Night Brewing | Atlanta, GA | mondaynightbrewing.com

The First Crowdsourced Beerd Ever: The Monday Night crew teamed up with Scoutmob, a local deals and "experiences" site, to have the public vote on the best name and 'stache for their next brew. People voted through Facebook and Fu Manbrew emerged victoriously. ¡Viva la Crowdstache!

BEERD 'Staches

FU MANBREW
ELGIAN STYLE WIT

HANDLEBAR
BELGIAN STYLE W

WALRUS
ELGIAN STYLE WIT

MONDAY NIGHT®
BREWING

NDS ARE OVERRAT

Pretty Things Beer and Ale Project | Cambridge, MA | prettythingsbeertoday.com

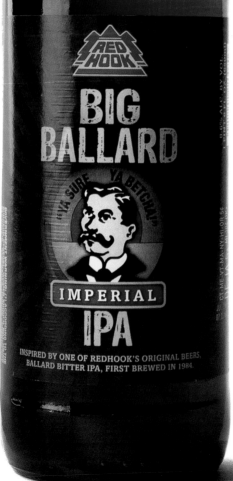

Despite his 20s-looking handlebar, Captain Ballard is more of an 80s child. Originally appearing on the namesake 1983 Ballard Bitter label, he was a fictitious character based on a photo Redhook's co-founder, Gordon Bowker, snagged from an apartment in college. The phrase "Ya Sure, Ya Betcha" was often heard by their brewery board member, Mark Torrance. Much better than the parlance of the time, "Totally, To The Max."

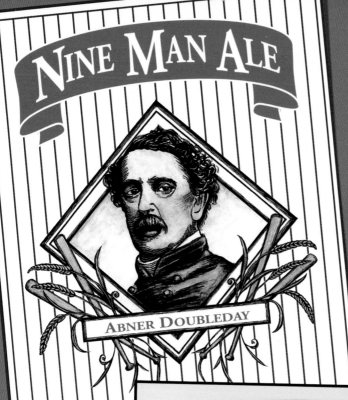

Nine Man Ale

Abner Doubleday

G...

Cooperstown Brewing
Milford, NY
cooperstownbrewing.com

Old Slugger

Pale
Ale

This Commander, though ruling class in name, is actually working class. It's a reference to a grain elevator building in historic downtown Stillwater, MN. The guy on the label is a rendering of one of the workers who carried sacks of grain there. When the brewery had its release party they held a moustache contest to get everyone in the spirit.

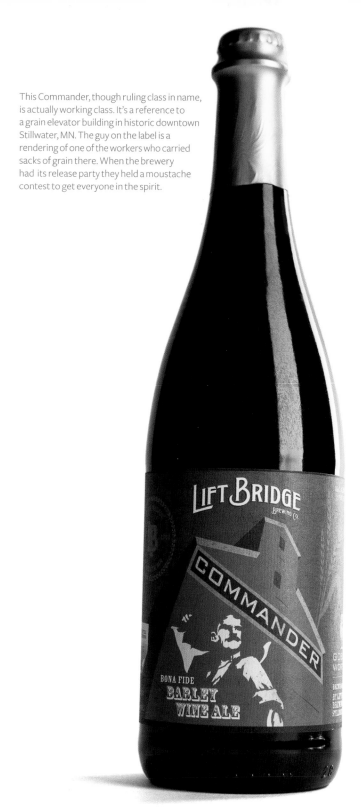

ligero
black lager

Flossmoor Station Brewing Co.
Flossmoor, IL
flossmoorstation.com

Avondale Brewing has a self-described obsession with Miss Fancy Elephant, the Queen of Avondale in the 1900's. After spotting her on their logo and even her very own label, Miss Fancy's Tripel, I believe 'em. Their website offers this backstory:

"Miss Fancy had a very special trainer named Mr. Todd. It has been said that Miss Fancy and Mr. Todd had a special understanding, and that she would not take instruction or direction from any other trainer than Mr. Todd himself. Mr. Todd was known for his intense affection for bootleg beer and whiskey, and being a sharing sort of bloke, he would allow Miss Fancy a few drinks as well. Together they would parade up and down the streets of Avondale, in the highest of spirits."

So, why the fingerprint on the face? "To show that despite the fancy clothes he wore back then (hat and tie) Mr. Todd was an animal handler and likely had dirty hands often." Details, folks. All about the details.

Avondale Brewing Company
Birmingham, AL
brewingcompany.com

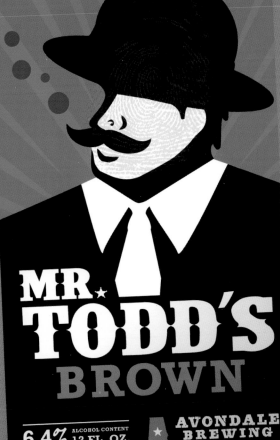

HANGAR 24 CRAFT BREWERY

NO.03

BARREL ROLL

RUSSIAN IMPERIAL STOUT
AGED IN BOURBON BARRELS

2011

PUGACHEV'S COBRA

December

§03

From pirates to gnomes and all lengths in-between. This burly batch of labels has all the beards that don't fit neatly into our strict, formal and highly-regimented Craft Beerd classifications. The stragglers and strays, if you will.

Photo-Illustrations by David Hodges/DNK Digital | dnkdigital.com

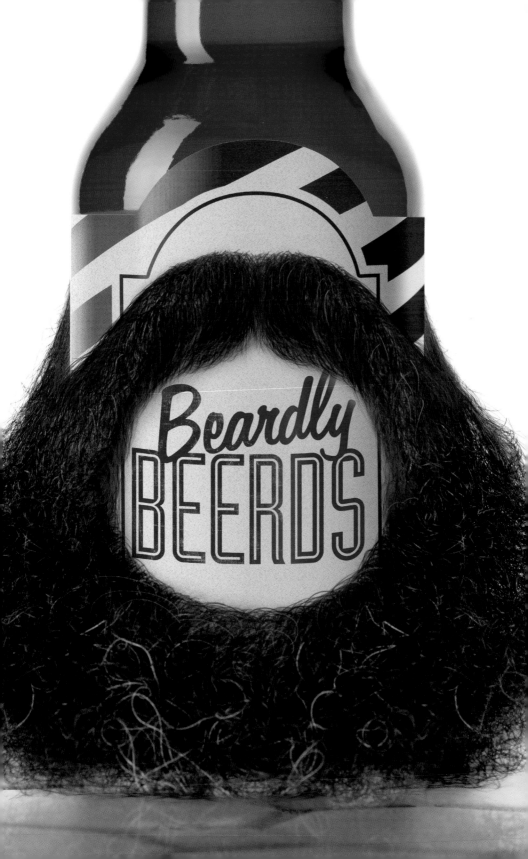

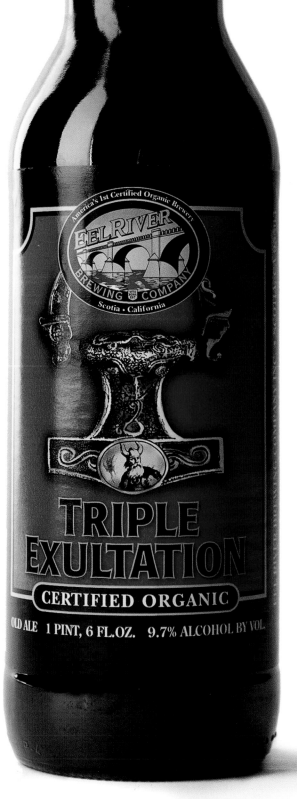

Beer'd Brewing Co. | Stonington, CT | beerdbrewing.com

WEYERBACHER
Blithering idiot

Barleywine ALE 11.1% ALC. BY VOL.

Weyerbacher Brewing Company
Easton, PA
weyerbacher.com

Illustrator: Sean Clark
Designer: Josh Lampe
ssmcreative.com

Beardly BEERDS

Middle Ages Brewing
Syracuse, NY
middleagesbrewing.com

Wizard's™
WINTER ALE

MIDDLE ◆ AGES
BREWING COMPANY
SYRACUSE, NEW YORK

This collaborative brew honors Geoff Dale: Man Child, Mother Bird, Minister of Mayhem, future President of The United States. A massive, hoppy imperial amber, Third Party Candidate goes down nicely after you chant: Vote Geoff Dale! Vote Geoff Dale! Geoff Dale!

1 pint, 6 fl. oz.
Alc. 10% by volume

50% Eagle Claw Fist Imperial Amber Ale
50% Loopy Oatmeal Red Ale

Brewed and Bottled by
Mercury Brewing Co.,
Ipswich, MA

FL CT-MA-ME-NY
OR-VT-5¢ DEP
MI 10¢ OK CA CRV

CLOWN SHOES™

Third Party Candidate

Imperial Amber Ale
50% Imperial Amber Ale, 50% Oatmeal Red Ale

THREE HEADS BREWING

This collaborative brew was created for the heat of the 2012 presidential campaign because they felt America needs a better option. So this is what they came up with. Yes, that's a Third Party Shocker being thrown up by Three Heads' founder Geoff Dale. Two in the ballot, one in the pint?

Clown Shoes Brewing
Ipswitch, MA
clownshoesbeer.com

Three Heads Brewing
Rochester, NY
threeheadsbrewing.com

Heavy Seas Brewing
Halethorpe, MD
heavyseasbeer.com

Winter Storm

Category 5 Ale

Shiver me timbers!

PRISON CAMP PILS

LAGER BEER

JAILHOUSE
BREWING
COMPANY
HAMPTON, GA

NET CONTENTS 22 FL. OZ.

Jailhouse Brewing Company
Hampton, GA
jailhousebrewing.com

Artist: Carsten Bradley
slumberground.com

Beardly BEERDS

Fabled Series

LIMITED EDITION

Fabled Series

Fabled Fermentation

Sooty
Brother

Grätzer Beer

1 PT. 6 FL. OZ.

Grimm Brothers Brewhouse
Loveland, CO
grimmbrosbrewhouse.com

Coast Brewing Company
Charleston, NC
coastbrewing.com

Ballast Point Brewing Company
San Diego, CA
ballastpoint.com

A note about Gnomes

Though not big enough (majoratively speaking) to merit their own chapter, the little guys from tall tales have shown up in a ton of craft labels. Whether they're deep in the mines or being attacked by the Easter Bunny they've always got some seriously solid beards.

Weston Brewing Company
Weston, MO
westonirish.com

RiverWalk Brewing Co.
Amesbury, MA
riverwalkbrewing.com

COLORADO MOUNTAIN TOWN CRAFT BEER

TOMMYKNOCKER
BREWERY

MAPLE NUT
BROWN
ALE

A FLAVORFUL BROWN ALE BREWED
WITH A TOUCH OR PURE MAPLE SYRUP

COLORADO

4.5% ALC/VOL   IBU 20

TOMMYKNOCKER HAS BEEN CREATING QUALITY, LAGERS & ALES IN THE CO...

Tommyknocker Brewery
Idaho Springs, CO
tommyknocker.com

Tommyknockers slipped into the mining camps of Idaho Springs in the 1800's with the discovery of gold in our mountains and streams. These mischievous elves, though hardly ever seen, were often heard singing and working. They guided many fortunate miners from harm's way and to the gold they sought.

RABBID RABBIT

IT'S NOT

NORMAL

THREE FLOYDS

Saison
ALE

Three Floyds Brewing Company
Munster, IN
3floyds.com

Artist: Kate Tastrophe
Designer: Zimmer

The name of Brasserie d 'Achouffe (La Chouffe Brewery) is a play on their town's name, Achouffe, which means "gnome". Naturally, all their labels have the bearded little creatures on them. This 2011 collaboration with New York's Ommegang is no different. And what else could it be named?

Solemn Oath Brewery

khlóros

Solemn Oath Brewing Company
Naperville, IL
solemnoathbrewery.com

Designer: Jourdon Gullet
jourdongullett.blogspot.com

PILOT
MOUNTAIN
PALE ALE

Foothills Brewing | Winston-Salem, NC | foothillsbrewing.com

One of the few Canadian craft breweries in this book, their Winter Beard is probably the most Canadian-y. As summed up by a note from the brewery:

″ What could be more reminiscent of a frigid Northern winter than a cozy beard and a warming Muskoka seasonal brew? ″

Muskoka Brewery
Bracebridge, Ontario, Canada
muskokabrewery.com

The labels for Bell's Kalamazoo Stout feature a series of regulars who frequented a bar in Kalamazoo called The Rex Café. Lad Hanka, a local artist, would arrive when the bar opened at 7 a.m. and in exchange for buying them a beer, they would let him draw them. The portraits were drawn in November, 1982 and have been the labels for this beer ever since.

Bell's Brewery | Galesburg, MI | bellsbeer.com

Artist: Ladislov Hanka

McGuire's Irish Pub | Pensacola, FL | mcguiresirishpub.com

You can guess that the bearded gentlemen is McGuire himself. What you may
not know is that he designed this himself, too. But why a dollar bill, you ask?
"Because we have over a million dollars on the ceiling of the restaurant."

Beardly BEARDS

Once again we've tapped six local artists to draft the labels for **Illustration Ale**, with a portion of the proceeds from each bottle supporting our GOOD FRIENDS at the ToonSeum.

Illustration Ale is a limited release bottle conditioned beer with a rich malt character. This is the final beer in our annual Festival of Darkness™ series. We released it near the Winter Solstice, so once you've made your way through the bottle, you'll also be more than halfway through the Darkness of Winter, with Spring just around the corner.

Thanks for supporting the ToonSeum, Local Art, and Local Beer.

Cheers- Scott

Why the Federal Government rejected the original design:
" The illustration ("X" OVER THE EYE) implies a physical effect that the product will have on the consumer. See 27 CFR 7.29 (e). "

What Jasen, the illustrator, said after he had to remove the "X" to pass American standards:
" I don't want to make anyone think this beer kills dinosaurs. "

East End Brewing Company | Pittsburgh, PA | eastendbrewing.com
Illustrator: Jasen Lex | awefulbooks.com

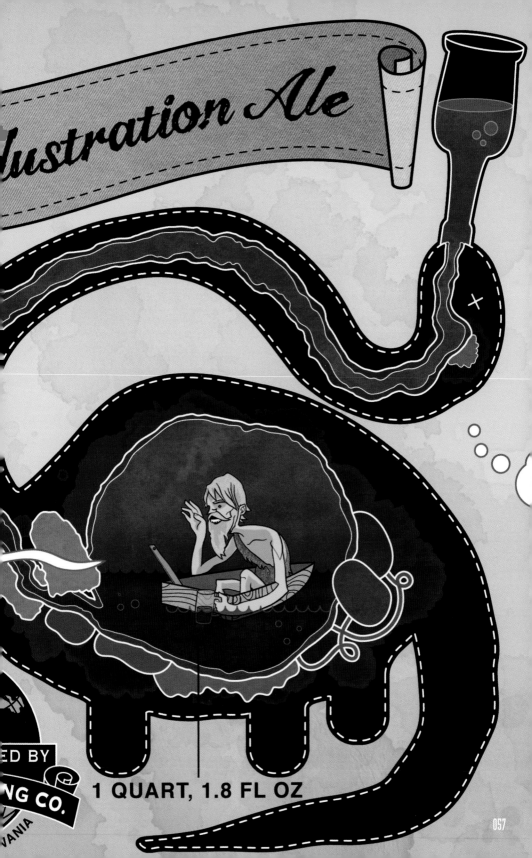

057

Microbrasserie Du Lac Saint-Jean | St-Gédéon, Quebec, Canada | microdulac.com
Illustrator: Patrick Doyon | www.doiion.com

Full Pint Brewing Comp
North Versailles
fullpintbrewing.c

Design: Phil S
philsethdesign.c

7,8%
alc./vol.

500
mL

GROS MOLLET

bière brune forte ● strong brown ale

MICROBRASSERIE DU LAC ST-JEAN

THE NEW
Classic
TEE

ITS SO SOFT YOU
WON'T WANT TO
WEAR ANYTHING
ELSE.

JESTER king

REDEFINE Luxury

www.jesterkingbrewery.com

Yeah, it's not a beer label. But the epic burlyness and classy use of mosaic
in this Classic Tee ad merits inclusion regardless. Especially since Designer/
Model Josh Cockrell got pronounced best beard at the 2011 Great American
Beer Festival by Denver Off The Wagon.

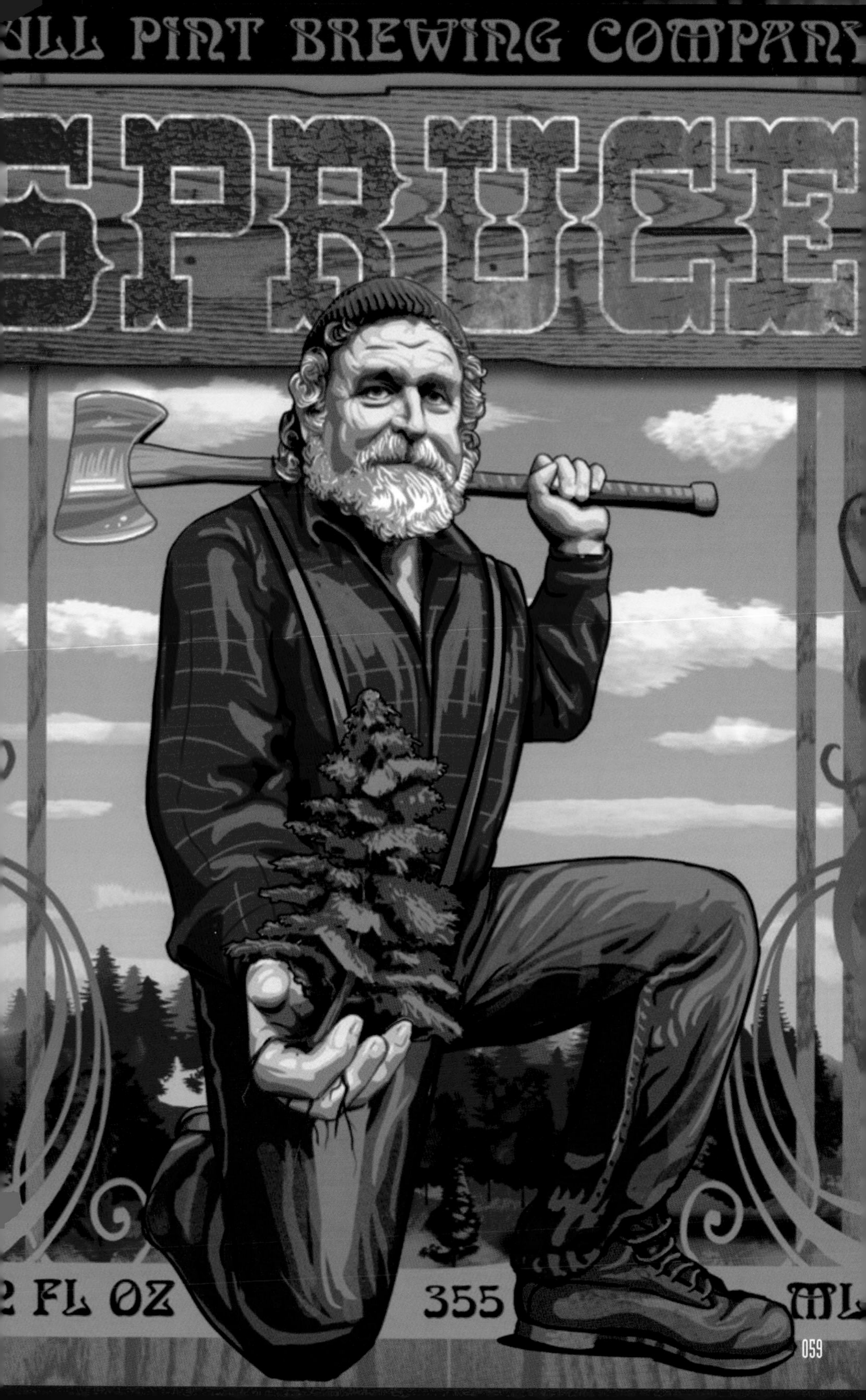

LL PINT BREWING COMPANY
SPRUCE
2 FL OZ
355
ML

ABOUT "THYME AFTER THYME"

FATHER THYME BESTOWS A DELICIOUS AND SEASONAL BLEND OF THYME AND BITTER & SWEET ORANGE PEEL TO WARM THE BODY AND SOUL.

BEST WHEN FRESH

DC BRAU®
THYME AFTER THYME
BELGIAN-STYLE WINTER ALE
BREWED WITH THYME

1 PT 6 FLUID OUNCES   9.0% ALC. BY VOL   BOTTLED IN: 2012

BREWED AND BO

PROUDLY
MADE IN DC

BREWING
BLUE POINT
COMPANY
LONG ISLAND

OLD HOWLING BASTARD™
BARLEY WINE STYLE ALE
10% ABV
1 PINT 6 FL.OZ.

Blue Point Brewing Company
Patchogue, NY
bluepointbrewing.com

LONG STRONG TRIPEL

750 ml
(25.4 fl.oz.)

Ovlova
Revol

www.boulevard.com/smokestack

No. 3

Beardly BEERDS

ILLUSTRATION ALE

Six local artists have conspired with THIS local brewery to bring you **Illustration Ale**, a limited edition, 700 bottle run of a one-time East End Brew. Each bottle bears handiwork of one of the six different artists who contributed to this project, and 2 bucks from the sale of each bottle will go directly to Pittsburgh's very own ToonSeum!

Illustration Ale is a bottle conditioned beer, with a rich dark malt character, spicy and nuanced, but without any actual spices added. That all comes from careful handling of our Farmhouse Ale Yeast. If you decide not to frame this bottle, you can carefully remove the label and return it to the brewery to collect your deposit. Or better still, bring it back and put it toward your next liquid art purchase.

Thanks for supporting the ToonSeum, and East End Brewing. I hope you enjoy the beer!

Cheers - Scott
EastEndBrewing.com

Label design by
Pat Lewis © 2010

**BUY A GOOD FRIEND
A GOOD BEER!™**

NET CONTENTS:
1 QUART, 1.8 FL.
OZ. (1 LITER)

BREWED AND
BOTTLED BY
EAST END
BREWING CO.
PGH,
PA.

GOVERNMENT WARNING: (1) ACCORDING TO THE SURGEON GENERAL, WOMEN SHOULD NOT DRINK ALCOHOLIC BEVERAGES DURING PREGNANCY BECAUSE OF THE RISK OF BIRTH DEFECTS. (2) CONSUMPTION OF ALCOHOLIC BEVERAGES...

HEADY-TOPPER

THE ALCHEMIST-VERMONT

ALE
ALC. 8% BY VOL.

OLDE BARTHOLOMEW

—BARLEYWINE ALE—

Yards Brewing Company | Philadelphia, PA | yardsbrewing.com

§04

With the exception of two solitary goatees (on a beatnik and an anthropomorphic onion), these labels are all of the moustache + goatee variety known as the Van Dyke. Named after Anthony van Dyck, a man who treated his facial hair like an artist. One of the 17th century, Flemish painter variety.

Photo-Illustrations by David Hodges/DNK Digital | dnkdigital.com

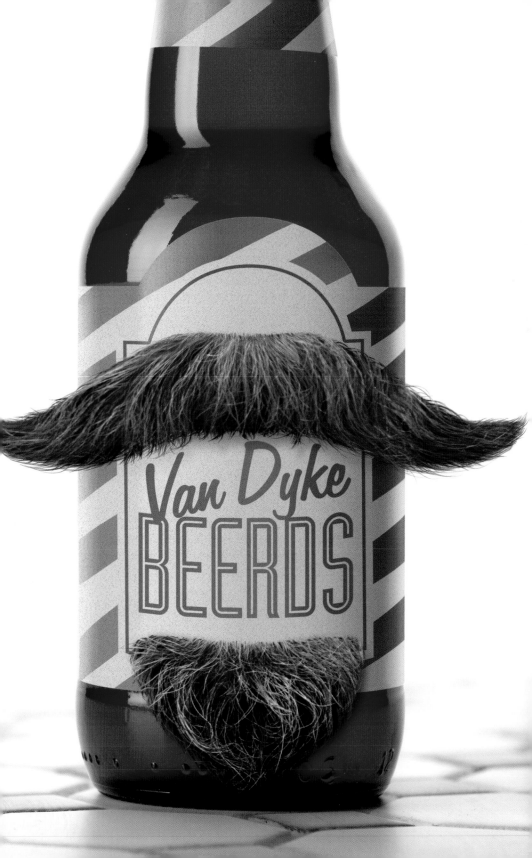

5,5%
alc./vol.

500
ml

VIЯE-CaPoT

bière blonde • blond ale

MICROBRASSERIE DU LAC ST-JEAN

Microbrasserie Du Lac Saint-Jean | St-Gédéon, Quebec, Canada | microdulac.com

Illustrator: Patrick Doyon | doiion.com

Hale's Ales Brewery | Seattle, WA | halesbrewery.com

The art was fashioned from an old fruit crate label branded "The Boss."
With the Spanish pronunciation of boss being "El Jefe," pairing
it with a German Hefeweizen is the only way it could possibly
be more bad-ass.

EL JEFE

ONE PINT,
6 FL. OZ

"THE BOSS"

WEIZEN
ALE
HALE'S ALES LTD. ~ SEATTLE

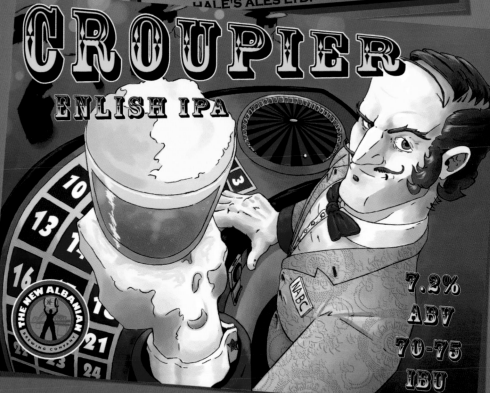

CROUPIER
ENLISH IPA

7.2%
ABV
70-75
IBU

New Albanian Brewing Company
New Albany, IN
newalbanian.com

Wild Onion Brewery
Lake Barrington, IL
onionpub.com

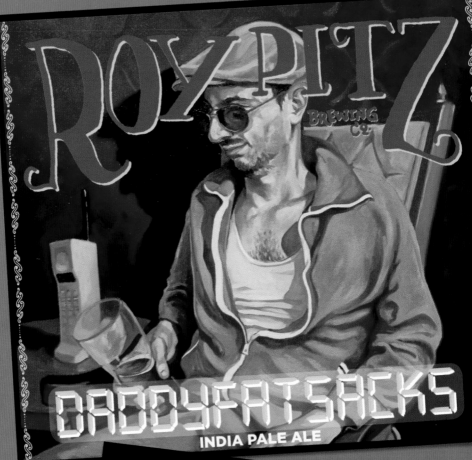

East End Brewing Company
Pittsburgh, PA
eastendbrewing.com

Artist: George Schill
georgeschill.com

Terrapin Beer Compa
Athens, (
terrapinbeer.co

Artist: Chris Pinkert

Fabled Series

Stout
Aged In
Bourbon
Barrels

The
Count

Imperial Stout

Grimm Brothers Brewhouse
Loveland, CO
grimmbrosbrewhouse.com

Grimm
Brothers

MOTHER'S BREWING COMPANY

Mother's Brewing
Springfield, MO
mothersbrewing.com

Three Blind Mice
NOT **YOUR** MOTHER'S BROWN ALE

BREWED AND BOTTLED BY
MOTHER'S BREWING CO.

5.5% ALC. BY VOL

BRETT & NO MICES

WESTBROOK
brewing co.

750 ML

1 PT 9.4 FL OZ

Ale aged in red wine barrels

6.5% Alcohol by Volume

Brewed and bottled by: **WESTBROOK BREWING CO.** Mt Pleasant, SC.

★ BRETT & NO MICES ★

"Instead of just one dickhead beer nerd complaining, there's is no hopefully enough or a customer base that some of these places will take notice."
-Old Time
Brettanomyces Bruxellensis is a wild, naturally ocurring yeast typically found in the Senne valley near Brussels, Belgium that grows on the skins of fruit and is considered a contaminant in some areas of the beer and wine industry but is desired ingredient in the making of the Belgian styles: lambic, Flanders red ales, geueze, and kriek. It has generally been attributed to giving a more barnyard, funky flavor to beers.

Best served at 45-50°F in a tulip or wine glass.

★ BOTTLED ON:

★ WWW.WESTBROOKBREWING.COM

Westbrook Brewing | Mt. Pleasant, SC | westbrookbrewing.com

Regarding the name and the quote on the back of the label:

From my understanding, the story goes that one night, Brandon "Old Time" Plyler had had one too many beers and was on a beer website or forum (likely, ratebeer.com) where they were discussing the popularity and availability of Belgian style beers made with these different funky wild yeast strains such as Brettanomyces Bruxellensis. And so a slightly inebriated Brandon made this post, talking about these styles of beer and how there is now hopefully more of a customer base for these beers and more breweries will start producing them. So we here at Westbrook were deeply moved by Brandon's eloquently put, and hopeful expectations. And so we decided to dedicate this beer to him. Even taking his beautiful southern pronunciation of "Brettanomyces" as the name of our beer.

—Colin Robison, WESTBROOK DESIGNER

FULL PINT BREWING COMPANY

HOBNOBBER

Full Pint Brewing Company
North Versailles, PA
fullpintbrewing.com

Design: Phil Seth
philsethdesign.com

074

12 FL OZ   355 ㎖

Wild Onion

Wild Onion Brewery
Lake Barrington, IL
onionpub.com

Brewing

Lake Barring

Mission Springs Brewing Company
Mission, BC, Canada
ssionspringsbrewingcompany.com

Van Dyke BEERDS

MR. BROWN'S

MASHING PUMPKIN

Winter Ale

650 ml   Flavoured Strong Ale • Ale Forte Aromatisé   8.0% alc./vol.

MISSION SPRINGS BREWING COMPANY

People's Brewing Company
Lafayette, IN
peoplesbrew.com

A male mermaid. Some dog whisperers. A Monkey's Uncle. And a leprechaun riding a cat. It's not the Animal Husbandry Scavenger List from Hell. It's the fine specimens of Barba Ferus Familia, Wild Beerds.

Photo-Illustrations by David Hodges/DNK Digital | dnkdigital.com

How Secret Stache Stout was born:

"I showed up for work one day with a moustache and everyone was like, "Where the hell did that come from?!" To which I responded, "It's a secret." To this day, no one can really explain how it is a man can grow a full Chicagoan moustache in less than 48 hours. But then, perhaps that's just it. I'm a man and I am from Chicago. Cheers.

—*Charlie Davis,* BREWER

Finch's Beer Company
Chicago, IL
finchbeer.com

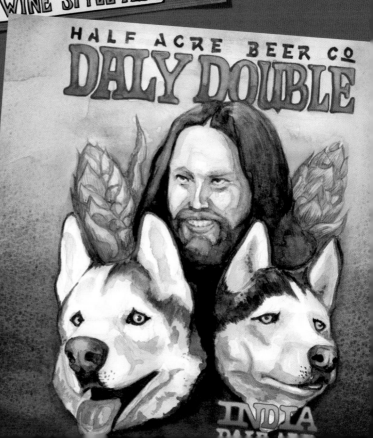

Half Acre Brewing
Chicago, IL
halfacrebeer.com

Artist: Phineas X. Jones
http://octophant.us

Wild BEERDS

""Daily Double is an India Pale Ale brewed in memoriam of a friend of Half Acre Beer Co., Terry Daly, who passed away ... Terry was a fan of music, geometry, his two Huskies, Moon & Luna, and amply hopped craft beer."

Short's Brewing Company
Bellaire, MI
shortsbrewing.com

SHORT'S BREW

UNCLE STEVE'S
IRISH STYLE STOUT
Leprechaun Magic is back.

BOTTLE CONDITIONED BEER

UNFILTERED

UNPASTUERIZED

50-55°F

Bonnie
THE RARE

1 PT. 9.4 FL. OZ.

AUSTIN, TEXAS

Jester King

Jester King Brewing
Austin, TX
jesterkingbrewery.com

Designer: Josh Cockrel

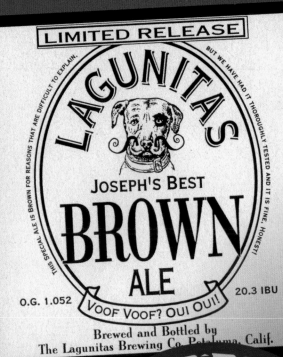

LIMITED RELEASE

LAGUNITAS

THIS SPECIAL ALE IS BROWN FOR REASONS THAT ARE DIFFICULT TO EXPLAIN.

BUT WE HAVE HAD IT THOROUGHLY TESTED AND IT IS FINE, HONEST!

JOSEPH'S BEST

BROWN ALE

O.G. 1.052   20.3 IBU

VOOF VOOF? OUI OUI!

Brewed and Bottled by
The Lagunitas Brewing Co. Petaluma, Calif.

CA Redemption Value

NET CONTENTS 22 FLUID OUNCES

THIS ALE IS NAMED FOR EDMOND JOSEPH SR., A PROUD SON OF THE FRENCH REPUBLIC AND A VERY GOOD FRIEND OF THE BREWERY. THE NAME JOSEPH HAS ALSO UNDERWRITTEN SOME OF HISTORY'S OTHER GREATEST ADVENTURES. IN 1429 EDMOND I FUNDED JOAN OF ARC'S DOOMED LIBERATION OF PARIS THAT LATER CAUSED HER TO BE BURNED AT THE STAKE. ED VI, ORIGINATOR OF THE ENDURING FRENCH CURSE: 'YOU SMELL LIKE ELDERBERRIES!', BACKED THE FIRST FRENCH 'CHUNNEL' EFFORT FOR LOUIS VIII. EDMOND MISTAKENLY SURFACED IN BARCELONA IN 1618, CAUSING THE BRUTAL 'THIRTY YEARS WAR'. TRAGICALLY, ON JULY 13, 1789, ED IX CLOSED A DEAL TO RENOVATE THE EMPLOYEE CAFETERIA AT THE BASTILLE. WORD IS, THE NEW LOOK WOULD HAVE BEEN VERY NICE. IN 1816 ED XI WAS ENGAGED TO SPONSOR NAPOLEON'S TRIUMPHANT MEDIA TOUR FOLLOWING WATERLOO. UNDAUNTED BY HISTORY, WE ARE PROUD TO BE PART OF THE HERITAGE OF THE JOSEPH NAME IN HISTORY. COME VISIT THE BREWERY AT 1322 ROSS STREET PETALUMA, OR CALL US AT: 1-707-769-4495.

Cheers!

Wild BEERDS

HAIR OF THE DOG

EST. 1993

BREWING COMPANY

LITERATE · SERIOUS · COMPLEX · BRAVE

PORTLAND OREGON

MICHAEL

FLANDERS RED STYLE ALE

Barrel Aged & Bottle Conditioned

YEAR **2009** MADE

12 FLUID OUNCES

ALCOHOL CONTENT 6.2% BY VOLUME

This Beer is produced in memory of Michael Jackson, the Beer Hunter. His writing has been an influence and guide to my beer journeys and inspired me to start my own brewery. Join me in drinking a toast to Michael Jackson, the most influential beer writer and critic who's ever lived.

Alan Sprints | Brewmaster

Hair of The Dog Brewing Company produces bottle conditioned beers which improve with age. We are dedicated to providing the beer lover with new and unusual beer styles. To learn more about Hair of the Dog Brewing Company and our beer styles, please visit us at www.hairofthedog.com

HAIR OF THE DOG

BREWING COMPANY

TRUE

WIS

BUOYANT

JOYFU

PORTLAND OREGON

084

FRED

Created to honor moustachioed beer writer and historian Fred Eckhardt.
We hope that Fred will inspire you to share your knowledge with others as Fred has with us.

Hair of the Dog Brewing Company | Portland, OR | hairofthedog.com

Petaluma has as many interesting events as Jack Passion has fiery-red follicles. From The World's Ugliest Dog Contest to Rivertown Revival, the annual Petaluma Whiskerino is a sure-fire standout. And probably one of California's oldest facial hair events, dating back to the Gold Rush days. For the last five years my wife and I have helped run and promote the event, growing it from the usual dozen hairy men to over 70 fine-follicled contestants from around California and beyond. We get local businesses involved by having them donate prizes. Including the fine folks at Lagunitas Brewing Company who, always generous with local groups, participate by hosting the after party and even helping judge the contest.

petalumawhiskerino.com

Wrepresentin': Justin Vorhauer, Don Chartier, Jezra
Photos by David Hodges/DNK Digital | dnkdigital.com

Petaluma Whiskerino contestant Reilly Williamson shows his
Lagunitas love with inkwork by the talented Adam Roach.

Left Hand Brewir
Longmont, C
lefthandbrewing.co

eworks Brewing Co. | Chicago, IL | pipeworksbrewing.com
st: Emily Cunningham | emilycunningham.com

aucus is the mythological stence of a being, both man d fish, a deity amongst re mortals. The only beer ng of such a name marries ld spicy Belgian yeast with ght citric American hops in way even the gods would lore. Savor this golden everage that can calm even e harshest seas.

BOTTLE ART BY:

Emily Cunningham
emilycunningham.com

Batch #

ww.pipeworksbrewing.com
12 Pipeworks Brewing Company
75 N. Western Ave. Chicago, IL.

BREWED AND BOTTLED IN CHICAGO, IL. BY
PIPEWORKS BREWING CO.

PIPEWORKS BREWING COMPANY

GLAUCUS

BELGIAN STYLE IPA

INDIA PALE ALE
BREWED WITH SPICES

1 Pint, 6 FL. OZ

ALC. 8.0% BY VOL.

East End Brewing Company
Pittsburgh, PA
eastendbrewing.com

Artist: Wayno®

"The recipe was developed by Brendan at EEBC, who bears some resemblance to the young Captain Beefheart, and as this is a smoked lager, they chose to name it after one of the Captain's songs*; the actual title is Blabber 'n Smoke."

–Wayno®

*Although the namesake song is off another of moustachioed Beefheart's LPs, The Spotlight Kid, Wayno® wanted to pay tribute to the album art of the era. What cartoonist can resist the creepy Cal Schenkel artwork of Trout Mask Replica? (I certainly could. That LP always freaked me out.)

IKEY'S
ICLE

Weizenbock Beer

Brewed and bottled by
EAST END BREWING CO.
PITTSBURGH PA

EastEndBrewing.com

§06

In theory, Western Beerds don't stray too far from the herd. They're either wooly, rugged or ruggedly wooly. But with the stories hinted at in the following labels' art, full of prospectors and gunslingers, you'll agree: there's gold in them beards. And them 'staches.

Photo-Illustrations by David Hodges/DNK Digital | dnkdigital.com

New Albanian Brewing Company
New Albany, IN
newalbanian.com

Tequesta Brewing Company
Tequesta, FL
tequestabrewingco.com

Southern Oregon Brewing Co.
Medford, OR
sobrewing.com

BOTTLED
NOV
2011

Our Finest Regards

...GED AND BOTTLED BY PRETTY THINGS BEER AND ALE PROJECT, WES...

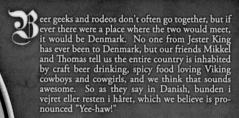

Beer geeks and rodeos don't often go together, but if ever there were a place where the two would meet, it would be Denmark. No one from Jester King has ever been to Denmark, but our friends Mikkel and Thomas tell us the entire country is inhabited by craft beer drinking, spicy food loving Viking cowboys and cowgirls, and we think that sounds awesome. So as they say in Danish, bunden i vejret eller resten i håret, which we believe is pronounced "Yee-haw!"

Jester King Craft Brewery is an authentic farmhouse brewery in the beautiful Texas Hill Country, on the outskirts of Austin. We brew what we like, drink what we want and offer the rest to those who share our tastes.

www.jesterkingbrewery.com

Beer Geek Ra...

ALC/VOL 10.1% **OG** 1.088 **FG** 1.0...

INGREDIENTS: *Water* (filtered Hill... and/or harvested rain), *Malted Barley*... crystal malt, brown malt, chocolate mal... chocolate malt), *Flaked Oats, Brow...* *Barley, Hops* (Millenium, Saaz, Cascade... *namese Coffee, Chipotle Pepper, Farmh...*

Suitable for Vegetarians

Notes: Imperial Oatmeal Stout brewed... chipotle peppers and Vietnamese co... bonated through re-fermentation in the...

STORE COOL & UPRIGHT.
REFRIGERATE MIN. 24 HOURS BEFORE OP...

BREWED & BOTTLED...
JESTER KING CRAFT BR...
AUSTIN TEXAS

The Big Beer of Texas

Scotch Ale, also known as a Wee Heavy is a big rich malty ale. When you open the bottle we recommend you pour it into two glasses and share it with a friend. As you drink the beer slowly the flavor will intensify and become more complex as it warms. This beer gets better with age, so buy 10 bottles and drink one a year for 10 years. Micro-Brewed and Bottled by Texas Big Beer Brewery, 400 County Rd. 3136, Buna, Texas

TEXAS BIG BEER BREWERY

RENAISSANCE
COWBOY
1 pint, 6 fluid oz.
ALE

GOVERNMENT WARNING (1) ACCORDING TO THE SURGEON GENERAL, WOMEN SHOULD NOT DRINK ALCOHOLIC BEVERAGES DURING PREGNANCY BECAUSE OF THE RISK OF BIRTH DEFECTS. (2) CONSUMPTION OF ALCOHOLIC BEVERAGES IMPAIRS YOUR ABILITY TO DRIVE A CAR OR OPERATE MACHINERY, AND MAY CAUSE HEALTH PROBLEMS.

Texas Big Beer Brewery | Buna, TX | texasbigbeer.com
Artist: John McKissack

Jester King Brewing | Austin, TX | jesterkingbrewery.com
in collaboration with Mikkeller | mikkeller.dk
Designer: Josh Cockrell

50-55°F

water
, dark
, pale
asted Viet-

malt,
, car-

GENERAL,
REGNANCY,
LCOHOLIC
ACHINERY,

UNFILTERED · UNPASTEURIZED · BOTTLE CONDITIONED ALE

Beer Geek Rodeo

STOUT BREWED WITH CHIPOTLE PEPPER & COFFEE ADDED

1 PT. 9.4 FL. OZ.

Jester King
Mikkeller

UNFILTERED · UNPASTEURIZED · BOTTLE CONDITIONED ALE

Whiskey Barrel Rodeo

STOUT BREWED WITH CHIPOTLE CHILES WITH KOPI LUWAK COFFEE ADDED & AGED IN OAK WHISKEY BARRELS

1 PT. 9.4 FL. OZ.

AUSTIN, TEXAS

Jester King
Mikkeller

Victory Brewing Company
Downingtown, PA
victorybeer.com

THE LEGEND OF 'HOP' WALLOP

Horace 'Hop' Wallop headed West a broken man. For in the City of Blues a Miss LuLu Belle Lager had left him thirsting for more. Drawn by wild tales of riches to be had in the gold mines, Hop pressed on westward. His last nickel spent on a prospecting pan, Hop's hunger got the best of him. Two fistfuls of barley and three of some wild and wayward hops tossed in a pan with some clear water was to be his meal. But sleep overcame him and he later awoke to a bubbling, cacophonous concoction. Overjoyed with the beautiful ale that he had made, Hop realized the secret of the green gold he had discovered in those fresh hops. Celebrated far and wide, Hop Wallop lives on in this vivid ale with his words, "hoppiness is happiness". Enjoy!

Bill
Ron   The Brewmasters of Victory

WWW.VICTORYBEER.COM · 8.5% ALC. / VOL.
BREWED AND BOTTLED BY VICTORY
BREWING CO., DOWNINGTOWN, PA

VICTORY®
'HOP'

WALLOP
VERY ALE HOPPY

12 FL. OZ.

William F. "Buffalo Bill" Cody was an army scout, showman, and entrepreneur who understood the power of "the brand" long before branding became part of our business lexicon. Our "Buffalo Bill Cody Beer" pays homage to the spirit of the man and the legend in a great tasting craft beer!

—Eric Bischoff, OWNER

Wyoming Territory Brewing Co.
Cody, WY
buffalobillcodybeer.com

alf Acre Brewing
nicago, IL
lfacrebeer.com

tist: Phineas X. Jones
tp://octophant.us

Mother's Brewing Company
Springfield, MO
mothersbrewing.com

MOTHER'S BREWING COMPANY
FOGGY NOTION
A BARLEYWINE STYLE ALE

BREWED AND BOTTLED BY
MOTHER'S BREWING CO.
SPRINGFIELD, MO.

10.0% ALC. BY VOL.

Tyranena Brewing Company
Lake Mills, WI
tyranena.com

"The Fargo brothers arrived
in Lake Mills in 1845, armed
with a strong collective will
and a pioneering spirit. The
Fargo family became leaders
in commerce, industry,
agriculture, civics and religion.
Through the years, these hard
working men and their families
shaped the character and very
essence of our beautiful hometown.
Their legacy endures in the buildings and
businesses they built and the civility they
brought to this city. In this same pioneering spirit,
we brew our Fargo Brothers Hefeweizen to
honor this "first family" of Lake Mills."

Tyranena Brewing

FARGO BROTHER
HEFEWEIZEN
Lake Mills, Wisconsin

" Bad Elmer represents the early settlers of the rugged southern Indiana Uplands: tough men and women with strong wills who lived off the land. It just so happened that a neighbor and good friend of the brewery looked just like we imagined those early Uplanders did, so he was a perfect fit for our Bad Elmer's Porter label. "

Upland Brewing Company
Bloomington, IN
uplandbeer.com

§07

"Barba non facit philosophum."
Which translates from Latin as,
"a beard does not constitute
a philosopher."

However, a philosopher with
a beard makes a brilliant Beerd label.

I'm still working on the Latin translation.

Photo-Illustrations by David Hodges/DNK Digital | dnkdigital.com

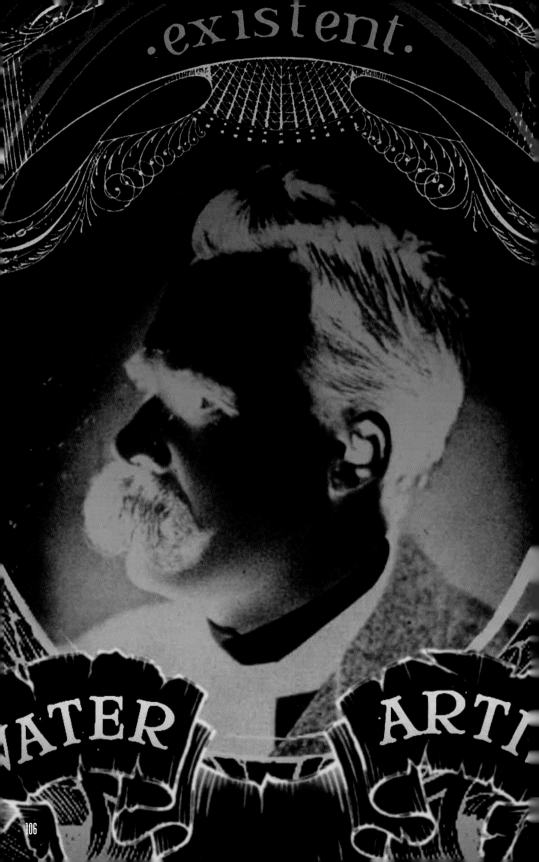

existent.

"And if you gaze for long into an abyss, the abyss gazes also into you."

—Friedrich Nietzsche

Stillwater Artisanal Ales | Baltimore, MD | stillwaterales.blogspot.com

Artist: Lee Verzosa | electricmadness.com

Regarding the Latin phrase on the label:
"It means, drink good beer with good people. This will be in English in the finalized version of the label. The problem is with the translation...The statement as is means, drink good beer with good people, inferring that the people are the vessels that are being drank out of. Thus our change to English.**"**

—*Adam Mills,* HEAD BREWER

BIBETE CEREVISIAM BONAM HOMINIBUS BONIS.

PROFESSOR

IPA

CRANKER'S BREWERY

5.9% alc. by vol.   12 fl. oz.

Shipyard Brewing Company | Portland, ME | shipyard.cc

Longfellow Winter Ale was first introduced in February 1995 to honor Henry Wadswor
Longfellow. The poet was born in the brewery's hometown of Portland, Maine (which,
1807, was still part of Massachusetts). The beer is still produced to this day, sporadica

North Coast Brewing Company
Fort Bragg, CA
northcoastbrewing.com

From the epically bearded label: "...Rasputin is probably best remembered for his dramatic exit. Having been deemed politically expendable, he was fed poisoned wine and tea cakes by his rivals. Surviving that, he was shot several times—whereupon he attacked his assailants. He finally succumbed when bound and stuffed through a hole in the ice to drown in the river Neva. Legends that attribute his tenacity to his appetite for Russian Imperial Stout are unproven."

Rushmore represents some of the greatest Presidential minds in American History. It also acts, for whatever reason, as a lightning rod for conspiracists. So here's a couple paranoid questions to mull over your next pint. Why do only two out of four Rushmore Presidents have facial hair? And did Lincoln have the first Strike Beard in history? He grew only the Southern portion of his facial hair, keeping the North nice and clean. Think about it. Not too hard though.

21st Amendment Brewery | San Francisco, CA | 21st-amendment.com

Illustration: Joe Wilson | joe-wilson.com

A grain of poetry suffices to season a century

American Porter

You may know José Julián Martí Pérez as a famous poet and Cuban patriot. But did you know he was also a revolutionary philosopher, a professor, a publisher, a political theorist, a translator, an essayist, and a journalist? What about how he was also part of the Cuban Freemasons? No?! Well, now you do. You're welcome.

§08

One of the more self-explanatory of Craft Beerd categories, it's also one of my favorites. That's why I reached out to a friend with the red beard by all other red beards are judged: Jack Passion. He's a World Beard Champion, two-time Petaluma Whiskerino winner and author of The Facial Hair Handbook.
Treat the following pages gingerly (that's red beard humor and I'm sorry).

Photo-Illustrations by David Hodges/DNK Digital | dnkdigital.com

Photo courtesy of Davon Slininger | davonslininger.co

"To me, the beard has always been about true, authentic self-expression. It is the outward manifestation of the inward mantra, "Be Yourself," at a primal, biological, and genetic level. It is proof that one has risen from the training grounds of boyhood into the brotherhood of man. A bearded man needs not prove himself to anyone, because his beard proves it to all who see it. "But what about red beards!? Why are so many beards red!?" people often ask me. Isn't it obvious?

There's a fire inside; It has to come out somewhere."

—*Jack Passion*

jackpassion.com

Three Heads Brewing
Rochester, NY
threeheadsbrewing.com

SAMUEL ADAMS®

TASMAN RED

RED IPA

6.75% ALC./VOL   ALE   1PT. 6FL. OZ.

Samuel Adams | Boston, MA | samueladams.com

TORCH

PILSNER

Foothills Brewing | Winston-Salem, NC | foothillsbrewing.com

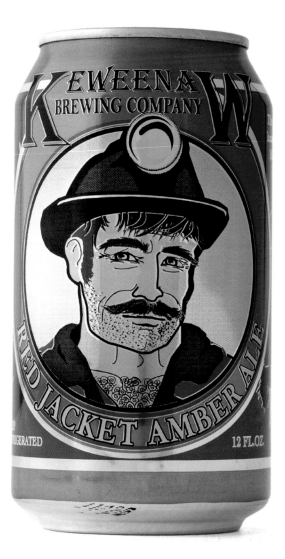

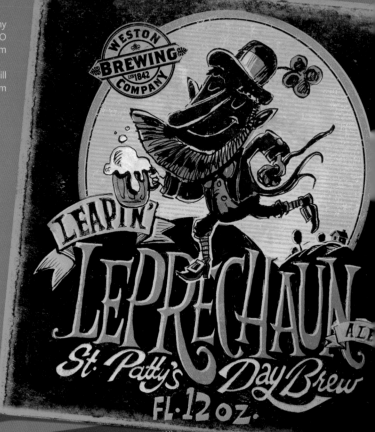

Weston Brewing Company
Weston, MO
westonirish.com

Illustrator: David Allen Terrill
davidterrill.com

Gray's Brewing Company
Janesville, WI
graybrewing.com

124

Magic Hat Brewing Company
South Burlington, VT
magichat.net

MAGIC HAT BREWING COMPANY

SOUTH BURLINGTON, VERMONT

4.5% ALC./VOL. ... OF ALE WITH SPRUCE ADDED

MAGICHAT.NET

FL82000131

Wooly

ESB
WITH SPRUCE

Big Red Beard Brewing Company
bigredbeardbrewing.com

Designer: Erik Teichmann
eriktdesign.com

BIG RED BEARD
BREW'NG COMPANY

RED ALE

TWIN

BEER CO.
ILLINOIS

Half Acre Brewing
Chicago, IL
halfacrebeer.com

Artist: Phineas X. Jones
www.octophant.us

127

Upright Brewing | Portland, OR | uprightbrewing.com Artist: Ezra Johnson-Greenough

This beer, Blend Love, helped commemorate Upright's three year anniversary and features a toasting, local Portland brewmaster, Ben Love of Gigantic Brewing.

BLEND LOVE

Upright Brewing

A barrel-aged beer with cherries and raspberries

© 2011 Throwback Brewery Brewed and Bottled by Throwback Brewery LLC, North Hampt...

THROWBACK
BREWERY

DIPPITY DO
American Brown Ale

5.7% ALC. BY VOL.

Throwback Brewery
North Hampton, NH
throwbackbrewery.com

HAND-CRAFTED IN SMALL BATCHES

DUHR XMAS BEER

REDBEARD CO. BREWING

This is where BS about how we make beer. It will fit into this space quite nicely I suppose. Oh Well, Just drink the beer...and tell people about it...cause I got kids to feed. This is where BS about how we make beer goes. It will fit into this space quite nicely I suppose. Oh Well, Just drink the beer...and tell people about it...cause I got kids to feed.

22 FL. OZ (650 ML). (ONE PINT 6 FL. OZ.)

WWW.REDBEARDBREWING.COM

9% ABV

OLD IRISH RED ALE

IT'S NOT NORMAL

Brian Boru

THREE FLOYDS

EYED COOPER

BARREL BARLEY WINE ALE

Uinta Brewing Company | Salt Lake City, UT | uintabrewing.com

Illustrator: Travis Bone | furturtle.com

RED LEGS

SCOTCH ALE

LED BY COAST BREWING CO

Extreme caramel malts with smoky undertones. Hops and Heather combine for bitter...

...acter.

1 PINT 6 FL OZ

1 PINT 6 FL OZ

1 PINT 6 FL OZ

1 PINT 6 FL OZ

BREWING **COAST** COMPANY

WWW.COASTBREWING.COM

ghland Brewing Company
heville, NC
ghlandbrewing.com

Weston Brewing Company
Weston, MO
westonirish.com

ustrator: David Allen Terrill
davidterrill.com

RUDDY GOOD.

§09

Kings and Kaisers.
Commanders and Czars.
Iron fists.
And stiff upper lips.
Beerds rule.

Photo-Illustrations by David Hodges/DNK Digital | dnkdigital.com

Three Floyds Brewing | Munster, IN | 3floyds.com

Artist: Dan Klien | Designer: Zimmer

THE FAMOUS
Narragansett

Narragansett Beer Company
Providence, RI
narragansettbeer.com

FEST
LA
SIN

MOTHER'S BREWING COMPAN

ALE AGED IN
BOURBON
BARRELS
IN COLLABORATION
WITH BROWN DERBY

Mother's Brewing Company
Springfield, MO
mothersbrewing.com

IMPERIAL
THREE BLIND MICE

Rush River Brewing Company
River Falls, WI
rushriverbeer.com

Ruling BEERDS

─ RIVER FALLS ─ WISCONSIN ─

UNFILTERED

BUBBLEJACK

UNPASTEURIZED

BUBBLEJACK

INDIA PALE ALE

FL **12** OZ

Rush River BREWING CO.

KEEP REFRIGERATED

BridgePort Brewing Company | Bridgeport, CT | bridgeportbrew.com

EPIC FLANDERS-STYLE RED ALE

Upland Brewing Company | Bloomington, IN | uplandbeer.com

„Gilgamesh was the King of Uruk somewhere between 2750 and 2500 BC, and almost certainly would have worn a beard. Our label shows him as he might have appeared during his epic journey in the wilderness."

Petrol Station
Houston, TX
@petrol_station

только не пытайся меня наебать

BEERD

PETROL STATION ★ 985 WAKEFIELD ★ HOUSTON, TX 77018

KNEE DEEP BREWING Co.
FINE CRAFT BEERS

McCARTHY'S
★ BANE ★

IMPERIAL RED ALE
8% ALCOHOL BY VOLUME | 80 IBU

Knee Deep Brewing Co.
Lincoln, CA
kneedeepbrewing.com

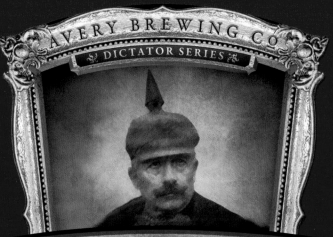

AVERY BREWING CO.

✤ DICTATOR SERIES ✤

THE KAISER

IMPERIAL
OKTOBERFEST
LAGER

AVERY BREWING
EST. 1993
BOULDER, CO

Avery Brewing Company
Boulder, CO
averybrewing.com

AVERY BREWING CO.

✤ DICTATOR SERIES ✤

THE CZAR

IMPERIAL
STOUT

AVERY BREWING
EST. 1993
BOULDER, CO

2nd REISING'S KAISER BEER ·

5.9% ABV

THIS OLD-FASHIONED PILSNER IS BREWED ACCORDING TO THE BEST PROCESS OF BREWING FROM THE CHOICEST BARLEY MALT & FINEST GRADE OF HOPS IS THOROUGHLY AGED AND IS GUARANTEED ABSOLUTELY PURE & WHOLESOME.

BREWED & CONSUMED AT

NEW ALBANIAN BREWING CO. INC.
NEW ALBANY, IND.

$4.25

40 IBU

New Albanian Brewing Company
New Albany, IN
newalbanian.com

RED MENACE

Big Amber

HALE'S ALES

Hale's Ales Brewery
Seattle, WA
halesbrewery.com

148

Tequesta Brewing Company
Tequesta, FL
tequestabrewingco.com

Ruling BEERDS

DER CHANCELLOR ™

Terrapin Beer Company
Athens, GA
terrapinbeer.com

Artist: Chris Pinkerton

Terrapin's "Big Daddy Vlady's" Russian Imperial Stout is Number 13 in our Side Project series of beers. Brewed under the strictest Socialistic guidelines, this Imperialistic Stout will be carefully monitored and allocated accordingly. Black as the coldest Siberian Winter's night, this colossal, viscous elixir will bring the hammer and sickle down on your little girly man's palet.

Spike's brewing words of wisdom.

Feel free to serve in shot glasses!

Na zdorovje!
Cheers,
SPIKE & John
Spike and John

TERRAPINBEER.COM

SIDE PROJECT VOLUME 13

SIDE PROJECT

TERRAPIN® SIDE PROJECT VOLUME 13

BIG DADDY VLADY'S RUSSIAN IMPERIAL STOUT

Pinkerton

BREWED BY: Terrapin Beer Co., 265 Newton Bridge Rd., Athens, GA 30607

149

Ironically, the facial hair style on this Three Floyds label, where the moustache connects with the sideburns, is called Friendly Mutton Chops. But look at those eyes. I think his last friend ended up in the Tandoor.

Three Floyds Brewing Company
Munster, IN
3floyds.com

Artist: Lance Laurie
Designer: Zimmer

BATCH NUMBER TEN FALL 2010

OLD WOODEN HEAD

AN IMPERIAL IPA

9.5% ABV

JOHN BELL HOOD

BREWED AND BOTTLED BY THE BURNT HICKORY BREWERY

CONFEDERATE GENERAL JOHN BELL HOOD WAS NICKNAMED BY HIS TROOPS AS "OLD WOODEN HEAD" AT THE BATTLE OF KENNESAW MT IN JULY OF 1864. THIS IPA IS AS TOUGH AND BITTER AS THAT OLD SON OF A BITCH WAS. SO HUZZAH!

Ruling BEERDS

Burnt Hickory Brewery | Kennesaw, GA | burnthickorybrewery.com

Three Floyds Brewing | Munster, IN | 3floyds.com

Artist: Ed Wisinski | Designer: Zimmer

DARK LORD

FLOYDS

КГЪЫШПΘΓ | Russian

ПЪЗУКΠΠΘΓ | Imperial

ПОК ШПКВ | Warlord

ВΘК.I | Dark

Dark Lord is a gargantuan Russian Style Imperial Stout, with a reverse cascading head that stars out billowing the color of burnt oil like the Dark Lord rising from the blood-primordial beginning of the Ri...

Named after renowned Maine native and Civil War hero Joshua Chamberlain.

Shipyard Brewing Company | Portland, ME | shipyard.com

Artist: Ken Hendricksen | civilwarartist.com

§10

James Dean rocked 'em in the 50s. Elvis swung 'em in the 70s. And Brandon dialed 'em in to the 90210 90s. Who's keeping cheeks in check for the new millennium?

Until we find 'em, these Beerd labels are giving us hope. And making the sideburns' late 1800s namesake proud—politician, soldier and railroad exec, Ambrose Everett Burnside.

Photo-Illustrations by David Hodges/DNK Digital | dnkdigital.com

As the only caffeinated beer in this book it's also worth noting the friendly-mutton-chopped man is MateVeza founder Jim Woods.

MateVeza | Ukiah, CA | mateveza.com

DRINK'IN THE SUNBELT

Mikkeller

COLLABORATION

Jester King Craft Brewery
Austin, TX
jesterkingbrewery.com

For this 2.9% ABV (a low-alcohol beer known as session beer) Jester King collaborated with Mikkeller, a Danish "gypsy brewer" who, rather than have his own brewery, brews at and with different breweries around the globe. Mikkeller's profile illustration is usually pictured somewhere on his labels but here it's been melded with Jester King's horned mascot himself.

Black Hatter™
Black I.P.A.

Ale

NEW HOLLAND
~BREWING~

WHITE HATTE
BELGIAN-STY
WHITE PALE A

NEW HOLLAND
~BREWING~

www.NewHollandBrew.com

ALE BREWED WITH WHEAT & SPICES

RYE HATTER™
Rye P.A.

Ale brewed with Rye

NEW HOLLAND
~BREWING~

www.NewHollandBrew.com

IMPERIAL HA
INDIA PALE AL

THE HIGH GRAVITY SERIES FRO
NEW HOLLAND
~BREWING~

www.NewHollandBrew.com

WESTON BREWING COMPANY
EST. 1842

O'Malley's
Festival Ale
IRISH STYLE BROWN

FLUID *12* OUNCES

THE HISTORIC WESTON ROYAL BREWERY WAS FIRST ESTABLISHED IN 1842 AT WESTON, MISSOURI.

WWW.WESTONIRISH.COM

BREWED & BOTTLED BY WESTON BREWING CO.
500 WEST ST., PO BOX 157, WESTON, MO 64098 (816)640-5235

0 94922 68184 3

Side BEERDS

Weston Brewing Company
Weston, MO
westonirish.com

ePort Brewing Company
Bridgeport, CT
bridgeportbrew.com

BRIDGEPORT®

OREGON'S OLDEST CRAFT BREWERY®

Bottle Conditioned Winter Warmer

humbug

6.4% ALC. BY VOL.

EBENEZER
ALE®

BRIDGEPORT BREWING CO
PORTLAND, OR

12 FLUID OUNCES

To clarify, having facial hair doesn't make you a freak. Pounding nails into your nostrils? Maybe. On the other hand, ask Samson about freakish hair and strength. I think Strongmen have the same follicles and that's their secret to lifting those heavy weights. Or maybe it's the tiny, striped unitards they're always wearing.

Photo-Illustrations by David Hodges/DNK Digital | dnkdigital.com

MALT BEVERAGE

"As a child it was always my dream to be made into an action figure. I ended up as a beer. I think that is a little better. And if that inner child starts to complain I can just drown him in alcohol.

I make my living performing strange stunts. Sword swallowing, Fire eating, Strait Jacket Escapes and other acts of the odd. In 2004 I started hosting the Sideshow in Coney Island. I would open the show with 'The Human Blockhead' Hammering a 60p nail into the center of my skull and living to laugh and joke about it.

The sideshow soon teamed up with Shmaltz Brewing Company and came up with Coney Island Lagers. Beers inspired by the performers in the show. The labels were designed by a tattoo artist Dave Wallen. Since the release of the beer the 'Human Blockhead' has gone through a few incarnations including being barrel aged in Buffalo Trace Kentucky Straight Bourbon Whisky barrels.

Since the beer has been released I had been able to travel to Beer Weeks across the US with Shmaltz. Performing sideshow stunts for beer lovers."

–Donny VOMIT
donnyvomit.com

Coney Island / Shmaltz Brewing Company
Saratoga Springs, NY
shmaltzbrewing.com

Finding The Right Taste Was Hard
Choosing The Name Was Easy.

Stevens Point Brewery
Stevens Point, WI
pointbeer.com

The goatee'd Conehead's actual identity is a bit of a mystery. Definitely a former employee in the 1800's, many believe he may've been a brewmaster back when Andrew Lutz owned the brewery, as there are pictures of him in a lab coat. His head, however, wasn't quite so pointy. But like any good beard, it's grown over time.

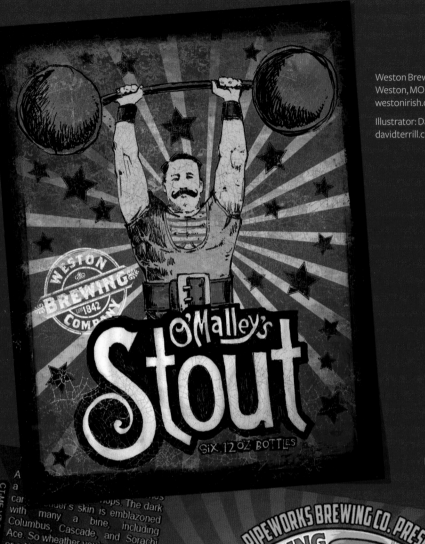

Weston Brewing Company
Weston, MO
westonirish.com

Illustrator: David Allen Terrill
davidterrill.com

Pipeworks Brewing Co
Chicago, I
pipeworksbrewing.com

Artist: Jason Burk
inkandleaddesigns.com

WESTON BREWING EST 1842 COMPANY

O'Malley's
Stout
SIX 12 OZ BOTTLES

A
a
car   hops. The dark
with   eader's skin is emblazoned
Columbus,   many   a   bine,   including
Ace. So wheather Cascade, and Sorachi
or a Nightshade, you're a Halloway
for with this carnival, you had better run,
Hoppy This Way Comes. Something

BOTTLE ART BY:
Jason Burke

ink&lead
DESIGNS
inkandleaddesigns.com

DRINK FRESH!
STORE COLD!

worksbrewing.com
peworks Brewing Company
Western Ave. Chicago, IL.

Batch #

PIPEWORKS BREWING CO. PRESENTS
SOMETHING HOPPY
THIS WAY COMES
IMPERIAL IPA ALE
1 PINT, 6 FL. OZ.

GOVERNMENT WARNING
GENER

Ladies & Gentlemen!
presenting

THE STRONGMAN ALE

CASCADIAN
STRONG
ALE

650 ml   Strong Ale · Ale Forte   8.0 % alc./vol

★★★★★★★★

MISSI
SPRIN
BREWING

Mission Springs Brewing Company
Mission, BC, Canada
missionspringsbrewingcompany.com

SAN FRANCISCO
BREWERS
GUILD

BREWED FOR
SF BEER WEEK

2012

SF STRONG ALE

San Francisco Brewers Guild
San Francisco, CA
sfbrewersguild.org

This tap sticker was a one-off created for the annual Lagunitas Beer Circus, held at the Petaluma brewery every May. They showcase everything from sword swallowers, burlesque entertainers, acrobats and every other flavor of freak. Throw in a couple dozen local breweries and an actual Big Top for an afternoon you'll never forget. Or ever remember?

Lagunitas Brewing Company
Petaluma, CA
lagunitas.com

§12

Monks have a lot of time on their hands. Probably why they brew beer and grow beards. Apparently, the same goes for Saints, Polygamists, Baptists, and Gandhi robots. Thank heavens.

Photo-Illustrations by David Hodges/DNK Digital | dnkdigital.com

SAINT ARNOLD

AMBER
ALE
HANDCRAFTED • MICROBREWED

Saint Arnold Brewing Company
Houston, TX
saintarnold.com

Brother David's Double
Abbey Style Ale

Brewed in a cloistered nook of remote Anderson Valley, this handcrafted Belgian-style strong ale may be the closest you'll ever get to heaven on earth. Made in very limited quantity, it is malty, tangy and a little wild, it is sure to raise your spirits. We suffered to brew this enormously complex beer so that you can enjoy it completely guilt free.

SOLAR POWERED BREWERY

Brewed from malted barley, hops, water, demerara sugar, and special trappist yeast

Ne... ...zed
F... ...enjoy ...55°F

Brother David's Double
Abbey Style Ale

ANDERSON VALLEY
BOONVILLE — CALIFORNIA
BREWING COMPANY

Anderson Valley Brewing Company | Boonville, CA | avbc.com

That "monk" is David Keene, owner of San Francisco's world-famous beer bar, Toronado. He's also part of the Anderson Valley Society for the Study, Proliferation and Advancement of Small-Scale Monastic Brewing Sciences and Technology. Or, AVSSPASSMBST for short. Just rolls off the tongue, right?

Brother Benjamin is named for the mystifying founder of the House of David [Religious Commune] in Benton Harbor, Michigan—just north of Greenbush Brewing Co. in Sawyer. Most of the House of David grounds still exist today; at the time, they had a zoo, two orchestras, bowling alley, ice cream parlor and a barnstormer baseball team that routinely annihilated major league teams. They are at least partially responsible for the fruit growing industry in Southwest Michigan, pallets, forklifts and automatic pinsetters at bowling alleys. They were a bright bunch, and facial hair in the style of Brother Benjamin only fortifies that sentiment.

Greenbush Brewing Company | Sawyer, MI | greenbushbrewing.com

Big Bad Baptist was named that because the state of Utah did not like the beer Jack Mormon (a previous coffee stout we made) so one of our co-owners decided to poke a little fun at his own Baptist upbringing and make them question their own decision to not allow certain brands into the state system. It was basically a free speech statement but those Baptists sure like coffee, too.

Epic Brewing
Salt Lake City, UT
epicbrewing.com

EXPONENTIAL SERIES

CLOWN SHOES

Clown Shoes Brewing
Ipswitch, MA
clownshoesbeer.com

Artist: Stacey George

LET MY PEOPLE GO
PALE ALE

Le Trou du Diable | Shawinigan, Quebec, Canada | troududiable.com

Illustrator: DOMiNiC PHiLiBERT | dominicphilibert.blogspot.com

That's Father Hennepin, the Belgian missionary who discovered Niagara Falls and the only waterfall on the Mississippi River, Saint Anthony Falls. This label has now been updated and features the silhouette of the padre in a boat cresting the falls. While it's designed beautifully, we're glad Ommegang let us give this O.G. version one more victory lap before being retired.

Brewery Ommegang | Cooperstown, NY | ommegang.com

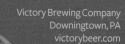

Victory Brewing Company
Downingtown, PA
victorybeer.com

• SEASONAL BREW •

The harbinger of Spring, our St. Boisterous is a refreshing draft of warmth and pleasure. Brewed in the Bavarian hellerbock style, this robust lager can seduce any soul with its exuberant character. Honest and sweet at heart, this well-seasoned brew is the product of flavorful German malts and whole flower European hops. Rich and golden in color, this celebratory beer brings with it the warmth of Spring, and the promise of glorious summer sun. Savor the good St. Boisterous!

Bill Ron

The Brewmasters of Victory

www.victorybeer.com

BREWED AND BOTTLED BY
VICTORY BREWING CO. AT OUR
SOLE LOCATION IN DOWNINGTOWN, PA

ST. BOISTEROUS
HELLERBOCK
A full-bodied **lager** *bee*
and robust

• SEASONAL BREW •

After crossing the Alps to their new home in Germany, the monks of St. Francis of Paula got down to the business of brewing beer. As early as 1634 it was recorded that they had created a rich, dark bock beer. Well-suited as the sustaining liquid that warmed them through the cold, late winter days, doppelbock remains a truly victorious brew today! Our St. Victorious is created of German malts and laborious double decoction brewing for a traditional taste, fresh as can be!

Bill Ron

The Brewmasters of Victory

www.victorybeer.com

BREWED AND BOTTLED BY
VICTORY BREWING CO. AT OUR
SOLE LOCATION IN DOWNINGTOWN,

ST. VICTORIOUS
DOPPELBOCK
A dark, rich **lager** *beer*

181

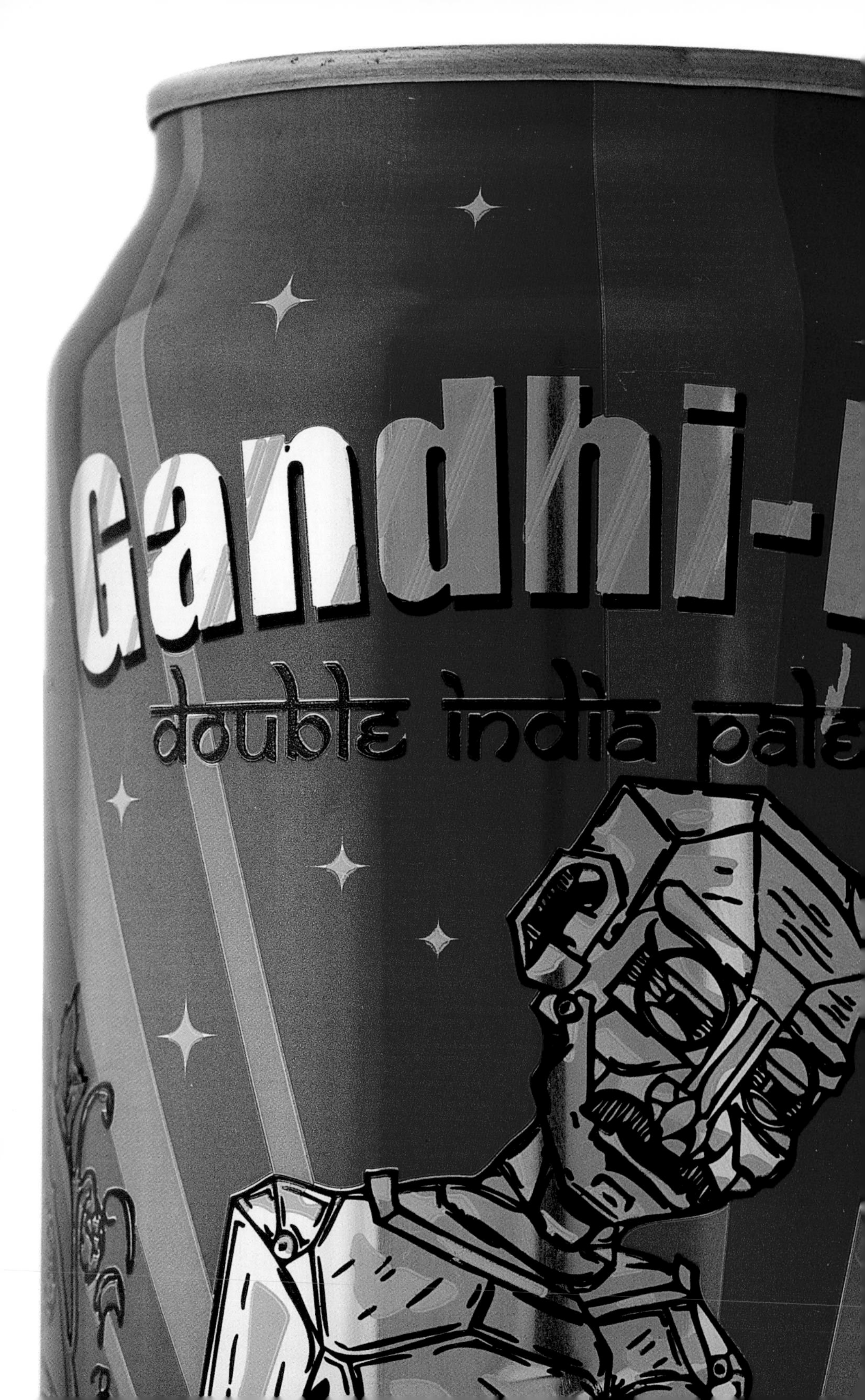
Gandhi-
double india pale

New England Brewing
Woodbrigde, CT
newenglandbrewing.com

Saint William
BREWERY

Weyerbacher Brewing Compa[ny]
Easton,
weyerbacher.c[om]

"...The mashing rake and the sword refer to William, Duke of Aquitaine, later know as Saint William. The sword is based on the actual sword my father gave to me on my wedding day, symbol that it now befalls to me to protect my house. The monk himself is based on my father, a little wink to the person who first taught me about beer, food, and sharing life."

Saint William Brewing Company
Warren, NJ
saintwilliambrewery.blogspot.com

WEYERBACHER
Old Heathen
IMPERIAL STOUT

8.0% ALC.

Shmaltz Brewing Company
Saratoga Springs, NY
shmaltzbrewing.com

L'CHAIM! TO LIFE!

HE'BREW®
THE CHOSEN BEER®

Shmaltz
Brewing Company

SAN FRANCISCO • NEW YORK

Heavenly BEERDS

water Brewing
troit, MI
waterbeer.com

ATWATER BREWERY

BOURBON BARREL AGED
Shaman's
PORTER
PORTER AGED WITH OAK BARREL SPIRALS

ATWATER BEER

BEER IS GOOD   ENJOY RESPONSIBLY

BREWED IN DETROIT

185

Stevens Point Brewer
Stevens Point, WI
pointbeer.com

12FL.OZ
(355mL)

St. Benedict's
Winter Ale

HAND CRAFTED

POINT • WELL M

Wasatch Beers
Salt Lake City, UT
utahbeers.com

WASATCH
BEERS

POLYGAMY
PORTER
Take Some Home to the Wive

www.utahbeers.com

The Lost Abbey | San Marcos, CA | lostabbey.com

§13

The devil takes many forms. Lucifer.
Beelzebub. Satan. And Kardashian.
They've all got well-manicured
moustaches but that doesn't mean
it's always part of the getup. Some
of the following labels prove there's
room for beards in hell, too.

Photo-Illustrations by David Hodges/DNK Digital | dnkdigital.com

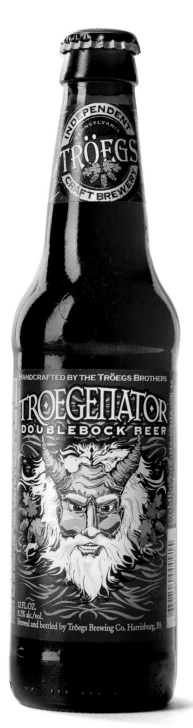

Tröegs Brewing Company
Hershey, PA
troegs.com

Devilish BEARDS

When searching for an iconic character for our Belgian Wit ale, designer Scott Pridgen came up with this White Devil. Our goateed Prince of Darkness is hidden in white with silver highlights and the beer itself is a classic take on a traditional beverage: quaffable fluffy white head with hidden spices on the nose and palate. Hail Satan!

—*Dave* RODGERS

Big Boss Brewing Co.
Raleigh, NC
bigbossbrewing.com

Design: Scott Pridgen
scottpridgen.com

Diabhal

Red Branch Brewing Company

Diabhal

Belgian Style
Ale Fermented
With Honey

5.2% ALC. BY VOL.

Rabbit's Foot Meadery
Sunnyvale, CA
rabbitsfootmeadery.com

Le Trou du Diable | Shawinigan, Quebec, Canada | troududiable.com

Illustrator: DOMiNiC PHiLiBERT | dominicphilibert.blogspot.com

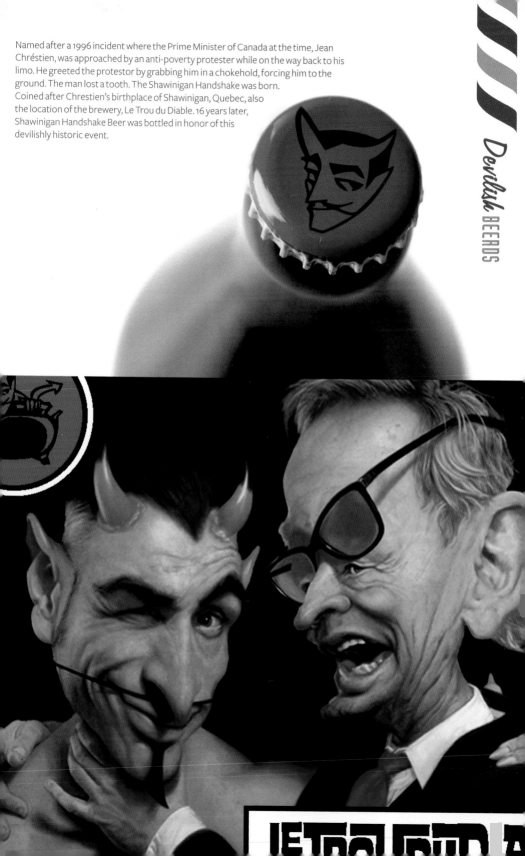

Named after a 1996 incident where the Prime Minister of Canada at the time, Jean Chréstien, was approached by an anti-poverty protester while on the way back to his limo. He greeted the protestor by grabbing him in a chokehold, forcing him to the ground. The man lost a tooth. The Shawinigan Handshake was born. Coined after Chrestien's birthplace of Shawinigan, Quebec, also the location of the brewery, Le Trou du Diable. 16 years later, Shawinigan Handshake Beer was bottled in honor of this devilishly historic event.

"European tradition says while St. Nick is busy delivering presents to good little boys and girls, Krampus hands out punishments to the bad. A fanged, goat-horned bully, the Christmas Devil uses sticks and chains to beat the naughty children."

Southern Tier Brewing | Lakewood, NY | southerntierbrewing.com

§14

Are they hiding some ▮▮▮▮▮▮▮▮▮▮
disfigurement? Did they forget
to ask permission? Are they about
to do the Humpty Dance? Or are they
▮▮▮▮▮▮▮▮▮▮▮▮ in their ▮▮▮▮▮▮▮▮ ?
Get the story behind the schnoz,
'stache, and ▮▮▮▮▮▮▮▮▮▮▮ .
Go incognito.

Photo-Illustrations by David Hodges/DNK Digital | dnkdigital.com

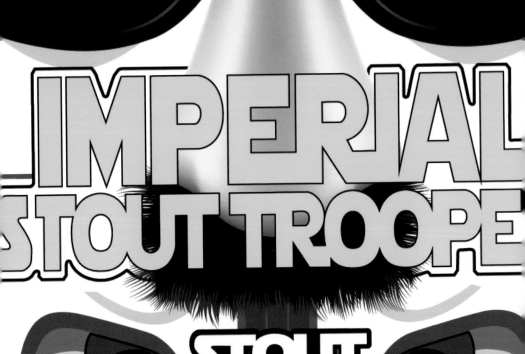

IMPERIAL STOUT TROOPE

STOUT

NEW ENGLAND
BREWING CO.

DRINK IT.   IT'S GOOD.

When Imperial Stout Trooper was first released it didn't have the Groucho glasses or 'stache. It also didn't have George Lucas' permission. A swift cease and desist changed that. Now you can only find pre-stache bottles in the rare, ISO trading circle appearance. Or see one at the world's largest private collection of Star Wars toys and memorabilia, Rancho Obi-Wan—in wonderful Petaluma, CA. Gotta love that town.

New England Brewing Company
Woodbridge, CT
newenglandbrewing.com

"Aren't you a little stout for a stormtrooper?"

ILLUST

SIX LOCAL ARTISTS HAVE CONSPIRED WITH THIS LOCAL BREWERY TO BRING YOU **ILLUSTRATION ALE**, A LIMITED EDITION, 700 BOTTLE RUN OF A ONE-TIME EAST END BREW. EACH BOTTLE BEARS HANDIWORK OF ONE OF THE SIX DIFFERENT ARTISTS WHO CONTRIBUTED TO THIS PROJECT, AND 2 BUCKS FROM THE SALE OF EACH BOTTLE WILL GO DIRECTLY TO PITTSBURGH'S VERY OWN TOONSEUM!

ILLUSTRATION ALE IS A BOTTLE CONDITIONED BEER, WITH A RICH DARK MALT CHARACTER, SPICY AND NUANCED, BUT WITHOUT ANY ACTUAL SPICES ADDED. THAT ALL COMES FROM CAREFUL HANDLING OF OUR FARMHOUSE ALE YEAST. IF YOU DECIDE NOT TO FRAME THIS BOTTLE, YOU CAN CAREFULLY REMOVE THE LABEL AND RETURN IT TO THE BREWERY TO COLLECT YOUR DEPOSIT. OR BETTER STILL, BRING IT BACK AND PUT IT TOWARD YOUR NEXT LIQUID ART PURCHASE.

THANKS FOR SUPPORTING THE TOONSEUM, AND EAST END BREWING. I HOPE YOU ENJOY THE BEER!

CHEERS - SCOTT
EASTENDBREWING.COM

LABEL DESIGN BY
JIM RUGG © 2010

BUY A GOOD FRIEND
A GOOD BEER!

East End Brewing Company | Pittsburgh, PA | eastendbrewing.com   Artist: Jim Rugg | jimrugg.com

ATION

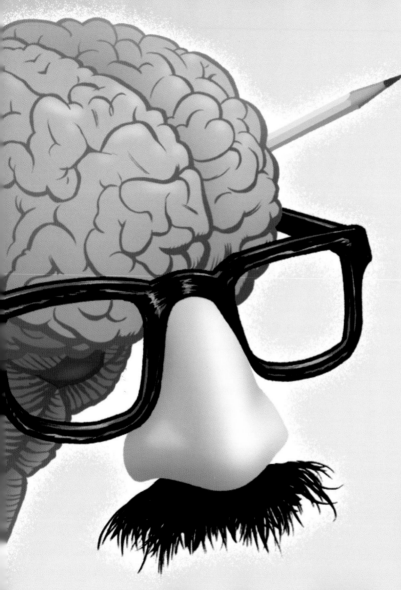

ALE

T CONTENTS: 1 Quart 1.8 FL OZ. (1 LITER)
REWED AND BOTTLED BY
ST END BREWING CO., PITTSBURGH, PA

rfish Head 75

Dogfish Head 75 Minute IPA
A bottle-conditioned India Pale Ale
with maple syrup.
7.5% Alc. by Vol. • 1 Pint 9.4 fl. oz.

The first incarnation of this beer was given the same name Dogfish gave the retrofitted 15 barrel tank used for brewing it, Johnny Cask. Naming aside, the Johnny Cash Estate felt the likeness of the imagery was, uh, walking the line.

Dogfish Head Craft Brewed Ales | Milton, DE | dogfish.com

§15

Q: Who gets more chicks in bands: the drummer, the guitarist or the singer?

A: The bassist.

I'm kidding, of course. That's ridiculous. It's the one whose Beerd goes to eleven, naturally. Rock on.

Photo-Illustrations by David Hodges/DNK Digital | dnkdigital.com

www.northcoastbrewing.com

ALC./VOL. 9.4%

BREWED & BOTTLED

NORTH COAST BREWING

FORT BRAGG, CA

Dig this. For every bottle sold of Brother Thelonious Belgian Style Abbey Ale (named after America's very own "Monk"), North Coast donates to the Thelonious Monk Institute of Jazz whose mission is to offer the world's most promising young musicians college-level training by America's jazz masters. And to present public school-based jazz education programs for young people around the world. All of these programs are offered free of charge to the students and schools.

North Coast Brewing Company
Fort Bragg, CA
northcoastbrewing.com

HOLLAND OATS

STILLWATER ARTISANAL®

Dutch Amber Ale

brewed and bottled by Bierbrouwerij Emelisse - Kamperland, Netherlands

emeli

Stillwater Artisinal Ales | Baltimore, MD | stillwaterales.blogspot.com
in collaboration with Emelisse | emelisse.nl
Artist: Lee Verzosa | electricmadness.com

"Holland Oats came up as a joke with one of my distributors in Chicago. Somehow it came up that he liked Hall and Oats and I said I should make a beer in the Netherlands called 'Holland Oats'... and I did!"

—*Brian Stillwater,* FOUNDER

Dark Horse Brewing Company | Marshall, MI | darkhorsebrewery.com

Designer: James Mestemaker | jamesmestemaker.com

THE KIND INDIA Pale Ale

50-55°F

BOTTLE-CONDITIONED STOUT AGED IN OAK BARRELS

FUNKMETAL
★ ★ ★ SOUR BARREL-AGED STOUT ★ ★ ★

WILD YEAST & BACTERIA

UNFILTERED UNPASTEURIZED

AUSTIN, TEXAS

1PT. 9.4 FL. OZ.

WATER),
ORGANIC
E MALT,
RYSTAL),
AND/OR
MHOUSE
AS HILL
ES

ONATED

URGEON GENERAL,
RING PREGNANCY
ON OF ALCOHOLIC
E MACHINERY, AND

Jester king

Jester King Brewing
Austin, TX
jesterkingbrewery.com

Designer: Josh Cockrell

*FUNKY

Jewbelation

HE'BREW THE CHOSEN BEER

SHMALTZ BARREL AGED RELEASE #6

Shmaltz Brewing Company
Saratoga Springs, NY
shmaltzbrewing.com

Three Floyds Brewing Company | Munster, IN | 3floyds.com

Artist: Tim Lehi | timlehi.blogspot.com

One of San Francisco's most badass and bearded tattoo artists, Tim Lehi, designed this special brew label for Three Floyds and their Viking Metal friends, Amon Amarth. "When Heimdall sounds the Giallar-horn this is the beer to be hoisted by the gods in anticipation of the coming battle." Indeed.

9353

BURNT HICKORY BREWERY

WE'D REALLY LIKE TO TELL YOU WHAT THIS IS BUT LIKE THE NAME 9353, IT'S YR GUESS

HINT 80 IBUS AMBER MALT OAK CHIPS AND PEACHES 16 PROOF

THE BURNT HICKORY BREWERY
2260 MOON STATION CT STE 210
KENNESAW GA 30144

LIMITED BATCH SUMMER 2011

The Burnt Hickory Brewery
Kennesaw, GA
burnthickorybrewery.com

BELL'S®

Le Pianiste Ale

Bell's Brewery
Galesburg, MI
bellsbeer.com

216

"DRINK TO BE SOBER"

ZZ HOP Triple IPA

AUBURN ALEHOUSE

I found out about this hidden gem of a brewery in Ken Weaver's Northern California Craft Beer Guide.

Brewmaster Brian Ford named this beer after bearded friend, loyal customer and hop-lover, Mike Sober. Yes, that's his real name. Hence the slogan on the label.

Auburn Ale House
Auburn, CA
auburnalehouse.com

ONE PINT

New England Brewing Company | Woodbridge, CT | newenglandbrewing.com

> "You can't be a real country unless you have a beer and an airline. It helps if you have some kind of a football team, or some nuclear weapons, but at the very least you need a beer."
>
> —Frank Zappa

Lagunitas released these beers in celebration of each Zappa album's 20th anniversary. They made it five brews/LPs in before Frank's widow, Gail, unexpectedly pulled the plug and reneged. Bummer.

§16

I think the best ad campaigns are the ones with conceptual legs. Ones that can last and evolve while always staying true to the brand. That's how I see these breweries' labels. None are consciously hairy that I know of. It just happens to be a recurring element. But it works. And it's why they're here...

Photo-Illustrations by David Hodges/DNK Digital | dnkdigital.com

Brewmaster John Maier

A little part of John in every bottle.

Rogue BREWERY

Newport, OR | rogue.com

One of Rogue's philosophies is "variety is the spice of life." You'll see on the following pages how the moustachioed Rogue on their labels has taken many different forms since their 1988 inception. The brewery says he is "no specific person, although there are many conspiracy theorists out there—George Clooney is the most common guess. It is simply the Rogue in Each of us."

If variety is the spice then beards must be the yeast—

Rogue recently made headlines with news about a beer made with beard yeast. Really. Here's the release:

Columbus may have discovered America but Brewmaster John Maier has discovered a new wild yeast that was developed from his old growth beard.

In cooperation with White Labs, samples were collected from Rogue's hopyard and sent to White Labs for culture and testing. Sadly all three samples proved incapable of producing a yeast suitable for brewing. As a joke, nine beard follicles were carefully cut from the beard of Rogue Brewmaster John Maier. The follicles were placed in a petri dish and sent in for testing.

To the shock of the experts at White Labs, the beard samples had produced a yeast strain that was perfect for use in brewing. Additional testing was conducted and confirmed that the yeast strain was not Rogue's current proprietary yeast, Pacman. White Labs' Chris White said "We were shocked and thrilled with this remarkable discovery."

John has been growing his beard continuously since 1978 and he has claimed that he will never cut it off. When told of the discovery, John said simply "It was in front of me the whole time and it only took two centuries and five decades to grow." The beard yeast is currently being used in test brews to determine the perfect style & yeast combination.

The beard beer, New Crustacean, will be released in early 2013.

ⓍGUE ROGUE

WORLD STOUT CHAMPION

1 PT. 6 FL.OZ.
650 ML.

7 Fl.

KESPEARE OATMEA   IMPERIAL STOUT

ⓍGUE

1 PT. 6 FL.OZ.
650 ML.

UNGER'S SPECIAL B

ROGUE

1 PT. 6 FL.OZ
650 ML.

Together We Co

YELLOW SNOW I

"Glen Ale is a strong, intensely hoppy ale brewed by Rogue Brewmaster John Maier in honor of Glen Falconer (1961-2002). Glen, who brewed for Steelhead, Rogue and Wild Duck is honored annually in Eugene, OR at the Sasquatch Brew Fest and the Sasquatch Brew Am in Portland, OR. All proceeds from both events benefit the Glen Hay Falconer Foundation, which is dedicated to furthering brewing education and supporting both the local and national brewing community. Glen was and always will be a true Rogue. He was a great brewer, a great friend and a great human being. Glen brewed and lived his life with an unrivaled passion. His beers are legendary—as is the man."

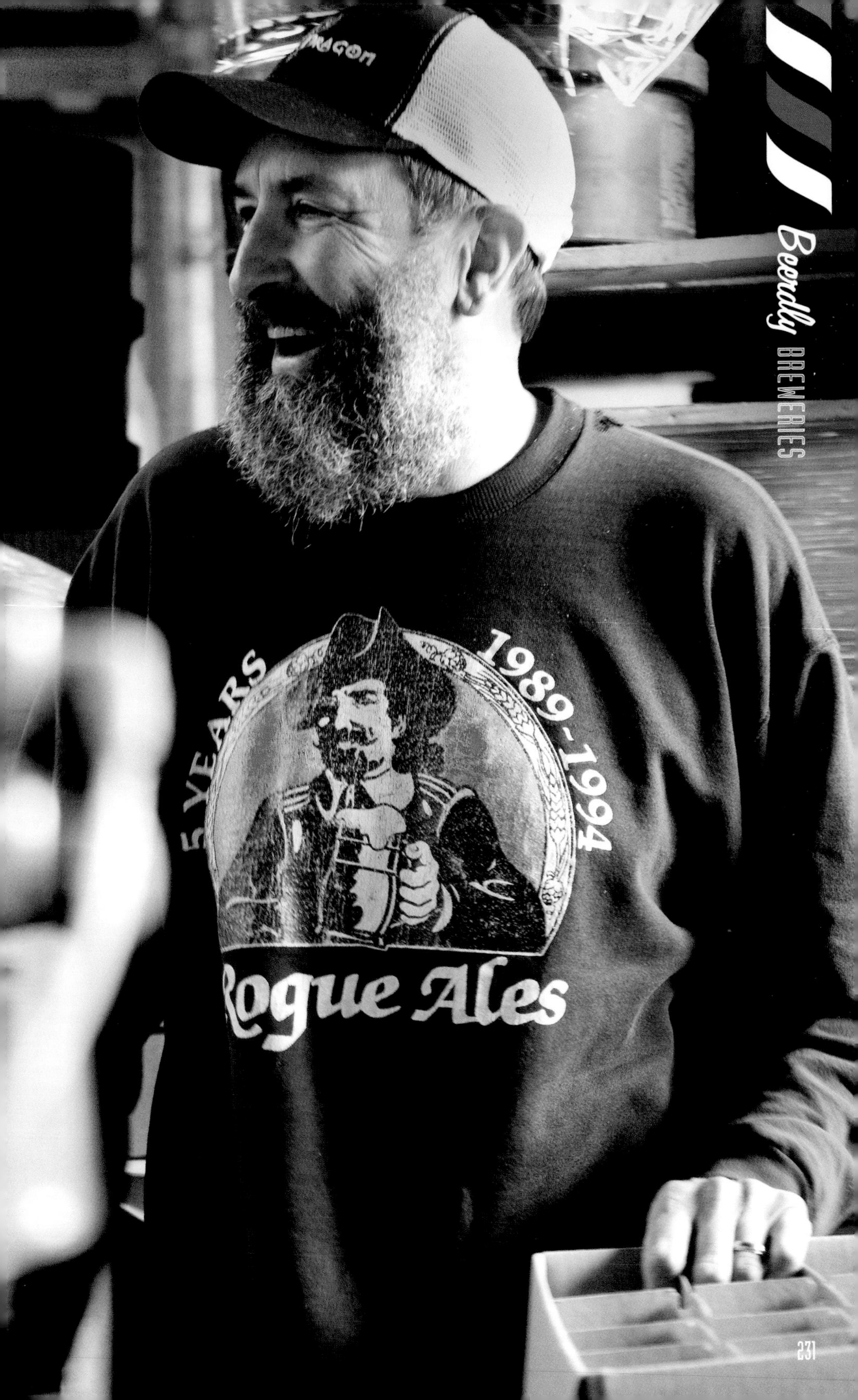
5 YEARS
1989-1994
Rogue Ales

TERRA I[N]

SIDE PROJECT

VOLUME

14

TOMFOOLERY

BLACK SAIS[ON]

[BRE]WED BY: Terrapin Beer Co., 265 Newton Bridge Rd., Athens, G[A]

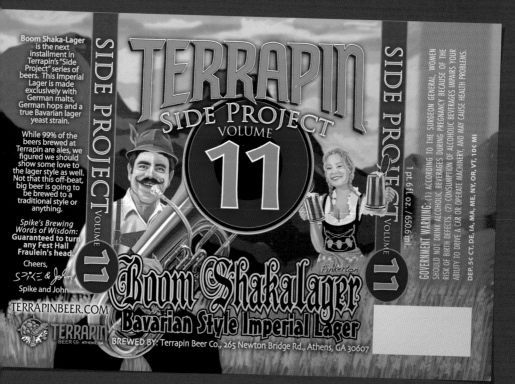

Boom Shaka-Lager is the next installment in Terrapin's "Side Project" series of beers. This Imperial Lager is made exclusively with German malts, German hops and a true Bavarian lager yeast strain.

While 99% of the beers brewed at Terrapin are ales, we figured we should show some love to the lager style as well. Not that this off-beat, big beer is going to be brewed to a traditional style or anything.

Spike's Brewing Words of Wisdom: Guaranteed to turn any Fest Hall Fraulein's head.

Cheers,

SPIKE & John

Spike and John

TERRAPINBEER.COM

Terrapin BREWERY

Talk about a concept with legs. Meet Mr Krunkles. AKA Captain Krunkles. AAKA Samurai Krunkles. AAAKA Indiana Krunkles. He's a recurring character in Terrapin's line of experimental one-off beers, The Side Project Series. In every appearance, there's fantastic art by Chris Pinkerton (of Grateful Dead, Rolling Stones, Bob Marley art fame) and equally fantastical stories that bring to life the interesting ingredients in each corresponding brew.

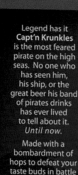

Legend has it **Capt'n Krunkles** is the most feared pirate on the high seas. No one who has seen him, his ship, or the great beer his band of pirates drinks has ever lived to tell about it. *Until now.*

Made with a bombardment of hops to defeat your taste buds in battle and all the black malt you can stand before walking the plank, this Black I.P.A. will make it worth going down with the ship.

Capt'n Krunkles... where is he?... I don't know... I don't know!

TERRAPIN
SIDE PROJECT
VOLUME
10

SIDE PROJECT VOLUME 10

SIDE PROJECT VOLUME 10

Capt'n Krunkles
Black India Pale Ale
India Pale Ale

BREWED BY: Terrapin Beer Co., 265 Newton Bridge Rd., Athens, GA 30607

TERRAPIN BEER CO. ATHENS, GA

1 pt. 6 fl. oz. / 650.6 ml.

Terrapin's **"Big Daddy Vlady's"** Russian Imperial Stout is Number 13 in our Side Project series of beers. Brewed under the strictest Socialistic guidelines, this Imperialistic Stout will be carefully monitored and allocated accordingly. Black as the coldest Siberian Winter's night, this colossal, viscous elixir will bring the hammer and sickle down on your little girly man's palet.

Spike's brewing words of wisdom.

Feel free to serve in shot glasses!

Na zdorovje!
Cheers,
Spike & John
Spike and John

TERRAPINBEER.COM

TERRAPIN BEER CO. ATHENS, GA

TERRAPIN
SIDE PROJECT
VOLUME
13

SIDE PROJECT

SIDE PROJECT VOLUME 13

Pinkerton

BIG DADDY VLADY'S
RUSSIAN IMPERIAL STOUT

BREWED BY: Terrapin Beer Co., 265 Newton Bridge Rd., Athens, GA 30607

ALC./VOL. 10.25%

1 pt. 6 fl. oz. / 6506.ml.

DEP. 5¢ CT, IA, MA, ME, NY, OR, VT, 10¢ MI

ALC. / VOL. 7.1%

TERRAPIN
SIDE PROJECT
VOLUME

17

Taking the Orient and
the rest of the world
by storm, Krunkles
returns! In this edition
of the bearded IPA
brewer's saga,
"Samurai Krunkles," as
he was once known in
the Far East, pulls out
all the hops from his
katana's sheath to
make this Asian flared
brew. While traveling
around the Pacific in a
souped up rickshaw
pulled by his trusty
side kick Cato,
Krunkles uncovered
unique brewing
ingredients such as
jasmine rice, jasmine
green tea and the
finest ginger the Orient
had to offer for this
Samurai master's ale.

Cheers! *Spike & John*
Spike and John
TERRAPIN
BEER CO. ATHENS, GA

SAMURAI
KRUNKLES

Pinkerton

ALE BREWED WITH GINGER AND WITH GREEN TEA ADDED
BREWED BY: Terrapin Beer Co., 265 Newton Bridge Rd., Athens, GA 30607

–1pt.16 fl.oz./(650ml.)

8 99539 00080 9

ALC. / VOL. 7.3%

The legend of Krunkles
lives on with number
15 in our Side Project
series of beers.
"Indiana Krunkles"
Wheat I.P.A boasts all
the hop adventure of
an American I.P.A. while
leading you on a quest
for malt and yeast
found in a traditional
German Hefeweizen.
Explore all the unique
flavor of this
unconventional
wheat
beverage
while
your
senses
take you on
a journey into
complete beer
nirvana.
We hope you enjoy
this audacious brew!

Cheers!
Spike & John
Spike and John

Spike's
brewing
words of
wisdom:
You
chose...
wisely.

TERRAPIN
BEER CO. ATHENS

TERRAPIN
SIDE PROJECT
VOLUME

15

INDIANA KRUNKLES
GERMAN STYLE WHEAT IPA
BREWED BY: Terrapin Beer Co., 265 Newton Bridge Rd., Athens, GA 30607

Pinkerton

1 pt. 6 fl. oz. / 650.6 ml.

8 58630 00102 3

CROOKED
FENCE
BREWING

IN YOUR
PORT SOON

Crooked Fence BREWERY

Garden City, ID | crookedfencebrewing.com

For a newcomer, Idaho's Crooked Fence comes out swingin' with bold and fresh illustrations that stand out from the first wave of craft brewers. Rough around the edges (in style, not execution), and in all the right follicles. Nice work, Kelly Knopp.

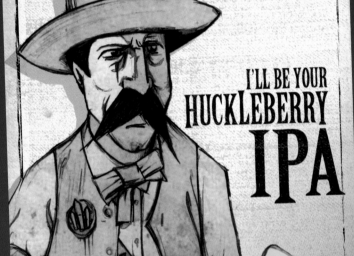

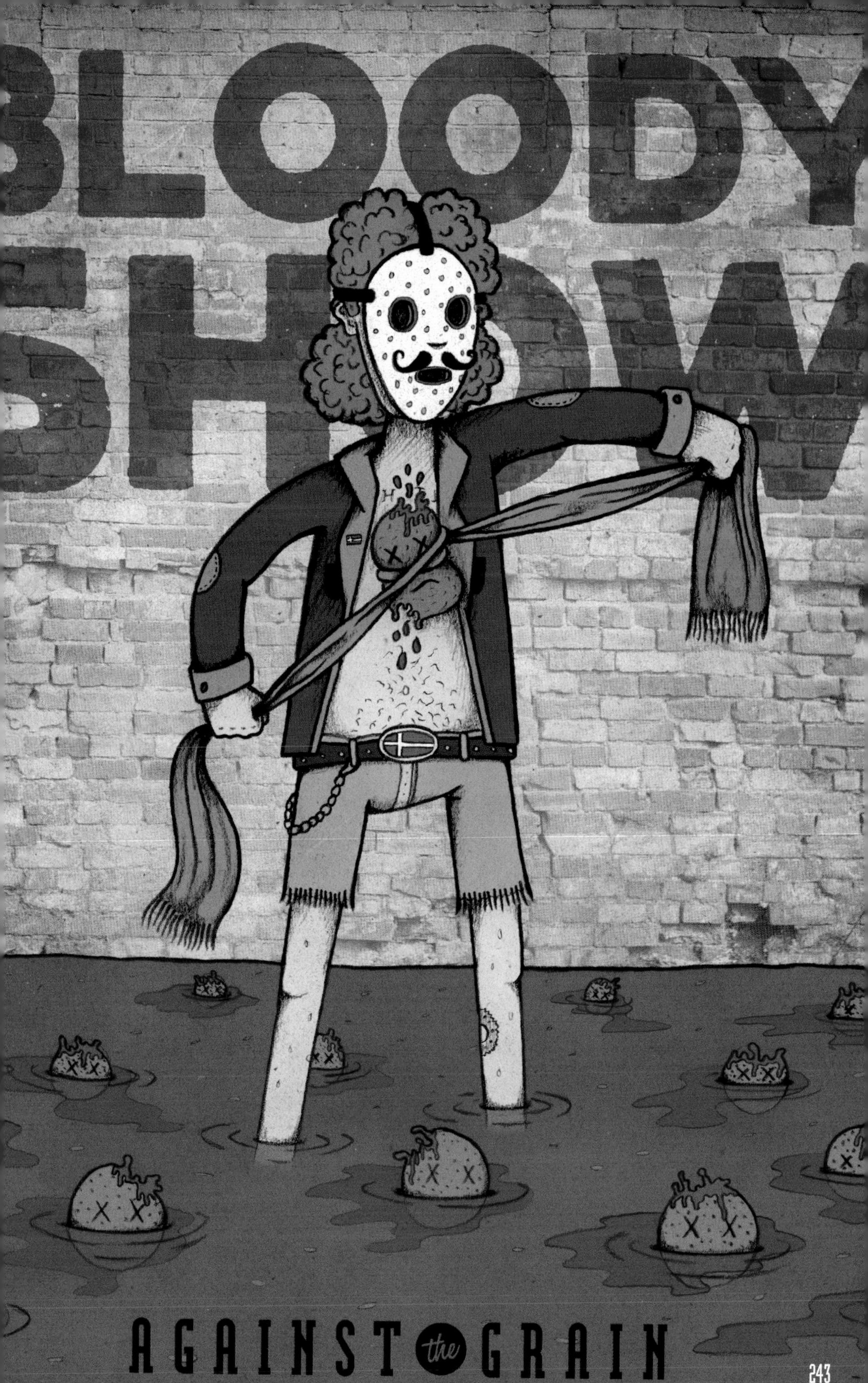
BLOODY
AGAINST the GRAIN

FAT HEAD'S
GÜDENHOPPY
UNFILTERED PILS

FAT HEAD'S
BATTLE AXE
BALTIC PORTER

FAT HEAD'S
HEAD HUNTER
INDIA PALE ALE

FAT HEAD'S
HAPPY HOLIDAYS
CHRISTMAS ALE

FAT HEAD'S
SORCERER
BELGIAN STYLE DARK ALE

FAT HEAD'S
PROHIBITION PAULY
PORTER

Fat Head's BREWERY Cleveland, OH | fatheadsbeer.com

I expected the namesake, fat-headed gentlemen on all of their labels to be a self-deprecating founding member or friend of the brewery. Turns out, he's way more meta than that. Get this: there is no one fat head. He comes from a term the founder, Glenn, and his friends in High School used to call each other. Whoa.

Founders BREWING

Grand Rapids, MI | foundersbrewing.com

"We don't brew beer for the masses. Instead, our beers are crafted for a chosen few, a small cadre of renegades and rebels who enjoy a beer that pushes the limits of what is commonly accepted as taste. In short, we make beer for people like us."

Though the original Founders people, Mike Stevens and Dave Engbers, stay relatively clean faced, a ton of people in the Founders Family are beardos. Which explains why so many of their beautiful labels have facial hair, too. It's just part of who they are. And their taste.

Curmudgeon's

BETTER
HALF

ALE BREWED WITH MOLASSES AND AG
N MAPLE SYRUP BOURBON BARRELS

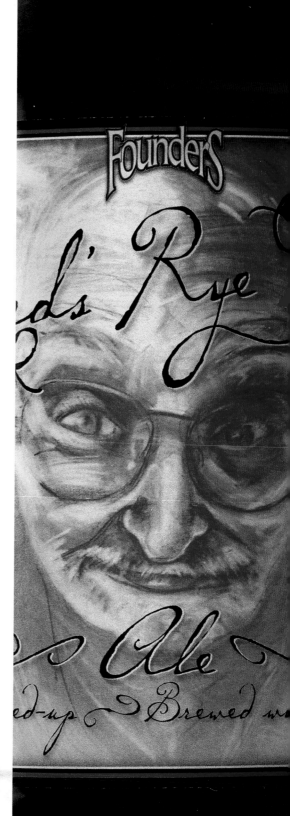

§17

I'm a huge geek for vintage beer can graphics. My Uncle Fred had one of the largest collections in his Chicago basement and I used to stare at them every holiday. They're burned into my retinas. Only time will tell if any of these modern Craft Beerd labels will endure in the same fashion. For now, take a peek at some favorites from the past. A few are actually still brewing strong today.

Photo by David Hodges/DNK Digital | dnkdigital.com

Old Reading BEER readingpremium.com

This beer dates all the way back to 1886 where it began brewing in Reading, Pennsylvania (home of modern day beer pen, Jay Brooks of brookstonbeerbulletin.com). Pre-prohibition they were known as Reading Brewing Company and post they were known as Old Reading Brewery. That is, up until 1976 when they were simply no more. Bought by Schmidt and essentially forgotten.

In 2010 a marketing agency named Ruckus acquired the brand rights and are working hard to revive Reading Premium and preserve the lushly-follicled legacy of the brand's old mascot, Gus. Even reissuing the original packaging. Pretty cool.

Here's a snapshot they put together for us of Gus through the years:

1934

1939

1939

1954

Olde Frothingslosh BEER

Mention this brand and most beer geeks will envision the curvy Olde Miss Frothingslosh (or Fatima Yechburgh to the über geeky). But before she graced cans of "pale stale ale with the foam on the bottom" there was another pretty face associated with the beer, the moustachioed Sir Reginald Frothingslosh IV. Too bad they were both phony.

In fact, the whole brand started as a promotional joke in the 50s by Pittsburgh radio personality, Rege Cordic. The ruse turned real thanks to the Pittsburgh Brewing Company who created dozens of humorous cans as gifts and collector fodder off and on through the 70s.

In 2011 the Pittsburgh Brewing Company held a design contest for what would become the next new Olde Frothingslosh label. 17-year-old Paige Sabedra used Reggie as reference for what would become inspiration for the winning design rolling out in late 2012. Her focus? Reggie's regal 'stache. No wonder it won.

OLDE
FROTHINGSLOSH™

THE FOAM IS ON THE BOTTOM!

National Bohemian BEER

Mr. Boh

NATIONAL
BOHEMIAN

"Oh Boy, What a Beer!"

National Bohemian
Baltimore, MD
nationalbohemian.com

August Schell Brewing | 1978

Dixie Brewing Co. | 1980

61 years haven't been too kind to this back-bar figurine. It used to hold up a tray in his left hand, which served up a real bottle of Rainier's Kräusen beer. As a Chicago native, I remember Old Style touting their "fully kräuezened" beers, too. Over time I realized that's just the German term for their lager carbonation process. Amazing what an umlaut and exotic name can do for marketing mystique.

Rainier Brewing Co. | 1951

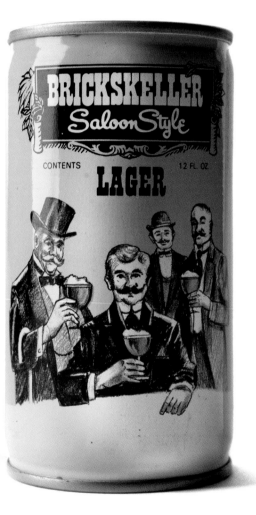

Pittsburgh Brewing Co. | 1977

Dixie Brewing Co. | 1977

CONTENTS 12 FLUID OUNCES

INTERNAL REVENUE TAX PAID

BEER

Cincinnati

THE BURGER BREWING CO.

BurgerBrau

CINCINNATI, OHIO, U.S.A.

NET CONTENTS 12 FL.OZ.

INTERNAL REVENUE TAX PAID

AMERICAN

Dutchman

BEER

MADE IN DETROIT

BREWED AND BOTTLED BY THE
AMERICAN BREWING CO., OF MICHIGAN
SINCE 1890

TBD Brewing | 194X

Brewery INDEX

Most of the bottles in this book were donated by the breweries themselves (the rest came out of my over-extended beer budget). So thanks to all who took the time to mail them out or dig up digital label files.

No breweries paid to be included. I reached out to them all myself and met a lot of kind people as a result.

See any good beerds lately?

Send 'em our way:
fred@craftbeerds.com

CB

SPECIAL THANKS to Jeremy Fish (sillypinkbunnies.com) and Jack Passion (jackpassion.com) for lending their beards and talents to the Craft Beerds cause.